HOPE

How Other People Endure

KAREN MARCHIONE

HOPE: How Other People Endure
Copyright © 2024 by Karen Marchione

ISBN: 979-8895312063 (sc)
ISBN: 979-8895312070 (e)

All rights reserved. No part of this publication may be reproduced, distributed, or transmitted in any form or by any means, including photocopying, recording, or other electronic or mechanical methods, without the prior written permission of the publisher and/or the author, except in the case of brief quotations embodied in critical reviews and other noncommercial uses permitted by copyright law.

The views expressed in this book are solely those of the author and do not necessarily reflect the views of the publisher, and the publisher hereby disclaims any responsibility for them.

Writers' Branding
(877) 608-6550
www.writersbranding.com
media@writersbranding.com

I dedicate this book to the people who shared their personal stories in the hope they inspire and help others through life and its challenges.

Be kind, for everyone you meet
is fighting a harder battle.

Philo

You are not alone.

You might feel like it after the loss of a loved one, a diagnosis no one wants to hear, or a personal struggle you are trying to overcome. It's a shock to one's system, and the world is suddenly turned upside down.

Life has changed forever.

Hope is the power of being cheerful in circumstances that we know are desperate.

Gilbert Chesterton

Contents

PREFACE ix

INTRODUCTION xi

MY STORY xv

Family

    1. MY SISTER, HELEN 1

    2. DR. TONY, MY HUSBAND 9

    3. RICHIE, MY STEPSON 19

Friends

    4. SIFU KEITH 29

    5. RON AND LAURA 39

    6. ANNA 49

    7. SALLY 55

    8. LINDA 79

CONCLUSION 101

ENDNOTES 105

PREFACE

How does one remain hopeful and endure life's challenges?

Webster's synonyms for *hope* are *faith, wish, dream, optimism,* and *confidence*. Synonyms for *endure* are *remain, persist,* and *exist*.

Does one's faith remain?

Does the dream persist?

Does optimism exist?

INTRODUCTION

Why am I writing this book?

I always felt I had a story to tell, but until now, life and other interruptions have kept me from sitting down to put my thoughts on paper.

When I was young and single, I left a job as an elementary school teacher to launch a career in commercial furniture sales. This adventurous move took me out of the bucolic country surroundings of Chester, New Jersey, where I had been living, and into the hustle and bustle of New York City. Youth gave me plenty of energy, but it also meant I was naive and learning something new about myself and the world every day.

Romance, of course, happened. Soon after moving to the city, I met my first husband, Thomas, who worked in a neighboring showroom. After a year of dating, we started a furniture business together, working out of our small city apartment, and the following year, we married. We poured most of our money into the business, so cash on hand was in short supply, but we put on a fine and joyful reception in my parents' backyard back in Jersey.

The time came to open our own showroom and move to the next level of our business. We found a location in a small building near the Architects and Designers Building in

New York City, a great place to sell furniture. Building out the showroom was a do-it-yourself project, and we received some design help from an architect friend. We were within days of opening, when life took a dreadful turn. Thomas died.

I was comfortable and successful in furniture sales, so I stayed with our business after the shock of losing my husband loosened its terrible grip on me. The work kept me going and kept me busy, and eight years later, I met Tony, a wonderful, dedicated physician, and married for the second time when I was thirty-nine years old. Five years later, our beautiful boy, David, was born.

After my son arrived, I stayed home to nurture and bond with my bundle of joy. As he grew and began school, I decided to go back to teaching. As a working mom, the frustrations and demands of the teaching profession, coupled with the responsibilities at home, brought on an onslaught of life's stresses. I felt I needed to find an outlet to relieve life's pressures. I needed to do something calming.

As good fortune had it, my son was taking lessons at a local martial arts academy. One Saturday morning, while I waited to pick him up after his black-belt class, the room filled with beautiful, relaxing music. A dozen or so men and women walked onto the floor and began moving in slow, rhythmic patterns and poses. It was a tai chi class, and that moment proved to be a moment of discovery that added some balance to my life. Additionally, Sifu, the master teacher, recommended a coach who became a lifesaver through her positive guidance, authenticity, and encouragement. She helped by offering another perspective and anecdotes that assisted me through many of life's challenges.

I hope the following stories of my life, my parents' struggle with their child's cancer diagnosis, my second husband's life-changing illness, and the challenging experiences of others are an inspiration to everyone.

Later, during the summer of 2013, my tai chi instructor, Sifu, was participating in a leadership seminar. He encouraged me to sign up and said it would further enrich my life. I was skeptical, but I decided to go. At the seminar, we were asked to write down our goals for the future. "If money didn't matter," a leader asked, "What would you do during your time left on earth?" I then realized my goal would be to write a book to help others get through difficult times similar to the struggles I had gone through. The idea of this book, *Hope: How Other People Endure*, was born in that transformational moment.

This book, now a reality, begins with my story and moves on to incorporate stories of my family members, including my parents; my husband, Tony; and my stepson.

Another individual I interviewed was my martial arts instructor, Sifu Keith, whose career was derailed by a car accident. He recommended I speak to Laura, whose husband, Ron, had been a dear friend of his. Ron had succumbed to cancer, and Laura was now a widow with two small children.

My friend Anna, with whom I attended a seminar promoting her Melanie's Boot Camp program, which she named in honor of her mother, described her intense personal life story of growing up in an abusive household.

As I drove home from a weekend seminar on mindfulness with my friend Sally, I heard her story of overcoming poverty, moving to the United States, and surviving abusive relationships.

The last story in this book is Linda's. I met her when

our boys were just a few months old. I knew there had been tragedy in her life, but I didn't know the whole story. After Linda read through my rough draft, she offered to write her story to be included in this book. Her story is of alcoholism and the loss of siblings.

When I mention to people that I've written a book, many want to know the title, and when I explain that my book is about people overcoming life's challenges, many begin to tell me about their struggles.

After each story, I include a few song lyrics to reinforce what I offer with a positive message.

One thing I know for sure is that we all have a story.

MY STORY

Decisions, decisions. We make so many every day. There are small ones: *What do I want to eat or make for dinner? What will I wear?* Then there are major ones: *Where do I want to live? Where do I want to go to college? What do I want to do with my life?*

People struggle with decision-making all the time. Someone once said to me that right or wrong, the important thing is to have the courage to make the decision.

I always planned to be an elementary classroom teacher, following in my mother's footsteps. I never really thought about doing anything else. At that time, special education was a new endeavor in schools, and I worked with small groups of students who did not pass the standardized testing. This was an ideal setting, yet I had envisioned teaching in mainstream classes. Then, in 1981, after five years of teaching, I started to think, *There's got to be more to life.* I was twenty-seven years old and teaching but not in the kind of classroom I wanted. I had lived on my own for many years, but when I knew I needed to make a career move, I decided to move back to my parents' home. Living with them would give me some time to think and figure out my next career opportunity. Coincidentally, the school system offered a career-change seminar (due to lack of enrollment), and I signed up.

The seminar focused on encouraging the attendees

to discover their interests and skills. As the leaders told us, one cannot go to an interview and say, "I'm a teacher," and expect someone to understand what that entails. They encouraged us to talk to people and let others know we were looking to change careers and were interested in speaking with their friends and family about their work. I met with people who worked for airlines, in the fashion world, and in the furniture business.

A fellow teacher called me one day to let me know her husband's furniture company was hiring. She asked, "Would you like an interview?"

I responded, "Of course!" I thought, *Wow, this is a job in the city, in a thriving industry.*

The interview went well, and I was sent to another office for a required personality test. Within a few days, I received a call offering me the position. I had one week to make my decision. I thought, *Here it is—do I change my life?*

I spoke to friends and established a list of pros and cons. One teacher said, "If it doesn't work out, you could always go back to teaching, and you would never ask yourself, *What if?*" That statement alone helped me make my decision. I took the leap and accepted the position. I was working in the epicenter building of commercial furniture manufacturers in New York City!

Five months went by, and I was enjoying my city life and the world of working and commuting. One day a call was put through to my desk, and the person on the line said, "Hi. This is Thomas Michael Seamus O'Halloran, and I need to take you to lunch." Little did I realize that a salesman from a neighboring showroom had told Thomas he needed to meet me, the new girl in the showroom down the hall.

Thomas and I went out to lunch several times, and one day he asked me to dinner with the offer to drive me home. After an enjoyable evening, we began the journey across the river to my home. As a typical city dweller, he thought he was driving to another country, though the trip took only an hour.

We saw each other often after that night; both of us were delighted with the possibilities of new romance but careful. Three months later, he asked me to move in with him. I had never lived with a man before. Life was good. Thomas had a terrific sense of humor yet a serious side to him. Two years later, we started our own business, a furniture sales representative group, and the future looked bright. I learned daily from Thomas about sales, whom to contact, and how to give a presentation. He had ten years' experience, and I had two. We weren't mining gold, but our prospects were good.

Two years after moving in together, we got married in a small ceremony and, to save money, held our reception at my parents' house in New Jersey. We had three incredible years together; our business grew, and our love flourished. But life doesn't always go as planned.

A year after our wedding, as we were installing carpet tiles in our new showroom, Thomas fell to the floor, and I couldn't wake him up. I called 911, and the EMTs showed up in five minutes. Not knowing many people in the city, I called my one friend and neighbor. She went directly to the emergency room to meet us. Thomas was not stable, and the elevator in the building was small. The EMTs worked on him for more than an hour before they transferred him to the hospital.

I kept waiting to see him. One EMT said there was a fifty-fifty chance of survival. I thought he didn't know what he was talking about. Thomas was going to survive.

A few minutes later, a doctor came out and said to me, "I'm sorry. He didn't make it."

I screamed as my world came apart in that moment. A kind nurse moved me into a separate room to regain composure. I was numb. My friend called my parents, who dropped everything and were on their way.

My family had endured loss before. They knew the pain that one encounters from the loss of a loved one. My sister, Helen, at thirteen years old, ten months younger than I, had suffered from cancer, neuroblastoma. For two years, she had been in and out of hospitals, until her frail body could not fight the battle any longer. Raised in a religious Christian home, I had listened to stories of miracles for years. Why couldn't one have happened with my sister? At fourteen years old, I had been angry with God and begun to question if he really existed.

On the other hand, my parents' faith got them through my sister's horrendous ordeal. They realized they had three other children who needed their love and guidance. My father said to me after Thomas died, "I don't know how you get through this. Your mother and I had each other to lean on after your sister's death." Yet I can't imagine the loss of a child.

In many ways, the loss of my sister helped prepare me for Thomas's death. This time, I wasn't angry with God, but I still didn't understand. A couple in my apartment building gave me the book *When Bad Things Happen to Good People* by Rabbi Harold Kushner. Reading that book made me realize God is not a vengeful God but a loving God. People get sick for numerous reasons, yet God is with us and puts people in our lives to help us through the difficult times. Only we can decide if we take the help or not.

There were challenging, questionable, and exciting experiences through the years at the company I continued to run. The business was our dream, and in my mind at the time, there was no choice but to keep the dream alive. The company grew as we set many new sales records. The 1980s were a time of growth, and the 1990s were a time to recharge.

As years went on, one manufacturer became our biggest success. With that success came the threat of losing my independence to them. After ten years of dedication and hard work, in 1996, I decided it was time to cut the cord. As a newlywed, my focus shifted to family and potential parenthood.

Life goes on. Nine years after Thomas died, I met and married Tony. How lucky am I to have had the love of those two wonderful men! Tony and I enjoyed married life, and as my biological clock ticked along, we tried and tried to have a baby. With the help of modern science, five years later, the joy of our lives was born: our angelic baby boy, David.

I was a stay-at-home mom for three years. It was a special time with my son. When David was three and ready for preschool, I started thinking about what to do in the next chapter of my life. As I thought about it, going back into the teaching profession seemed like the perfect decision for me. I had always used a lesson-plan format when giving sales presentations, and having a child presented a whole new perspective on education. I'd developed a new level of understanding of children. For example, I'd learned children understand the art of negotiation very early in their development. So at forty-nine years old, I made my way back into the school system, adapting to a new generation of students, along with continued improvements in special education.

Life has an amazing way of coming full circle.

There were a few more curveballs coming my way. Tony, my husband, was diagnosed with Parkinson's disease shortly after our baby was born. He was told he had five good years. As a knowledgeable and brilliant doctor, he took control of his diagnosis. He read and studied about the medications and the current theories. He did well for fifteen years and then declined.

As the disease progressed, there was an added component to Parkinson's called dystonia. This disorder is characterized by twisting and involuntary muscle contractions. The tremendous pain he experiences is beyond what a human being should be exposed to. As I try to help, I pray for peace in his body. How one person can endure this torture is unknown to me, yet he has a determination and a powerful will to survive. He continues to work because, as he says, "Being a doctor is who I am; it's not just a job." After his diagnosis, he didn't complain and worried more about David and me. He is truly remarkable.

We are now pursuing deep brain stimulation (DBS), which is credited with improving the quality of life, giving us renewed hope.

As I mentioned earlier, a few years ago, I began practicing tai chi to maintain more balance in my life, and my instructor, Sifu, was participating in a leadership seminar during the summer of 2013 and encouraged me to sign up. He said it would change my life. I was skeptical, yet I decided to go. It did change my perspective and gave me renewed energy in striving to be authentic and congruent in all aspects of life. During the course of the weekend, we attendees were asked to examine our essence and leave ego behind.

Now, at sixty years old, I feel I am living in the present moment, conscious of what's important. To continue this positive path and get through the daily challenges of life, I do tai chi, pray, and read lots of books. A few of my favorites are *A Return to Love* and *Illuminata: A Return to Prayer* by Marianne Williamson, *The Four Agreements* by Don Miguel Ruiz, and *Help, Thanks, Wow* by Anne LaMotte.

Throughout my day, I try to do things with love and positive energy and not react to anger. Don Miguel Ruiz's four agreements are a constant mantra:

1. Be impeccable with your word.
2. Don't take anything personally.
3. Don't make assumptions.
4. Always do your best.

FAMILY

1

MY SISTER, HELEN

A Story of Faith and Love

One day not too long ago, I was searching through old photos and cards and came upon a valentine for my parents from Helen. She had included the following poem. I'm not sure if she wrote this or copied it, but it is definitely an expression of her thoughts.

> Please don't call me shut-in
> When my eyes can see a star
> My ears can hear soft music
> My soul can travel far.
>
> Nothing can shut me in
> As long as God is near
> He tells me of His love
> And takes away my fear.
>
> I'm really not a shut-in
> Though I may be confined
> Within these hospital walls
> I can travel with my mind.

I spoke with my parents about the card and about Helen's life, and they created a portrait of my dear sister that is indelible. Here is some of what they told me.

In August 1966, Helen was an adorable freckle-faced eleven-year-old with auburn hair, ready for life's next chapter as she began middle school. Seventh grade was in the junior high school in a neighboring town. Just before Labor Day, the new incoming students had an orientation prior to the other students' arrival. Helen got on the bus, went to the school, received her schedule, and met her teachers. On the return home, walking from the bus stop, which was about a half mile from the house, she had tremendous difficulty in walking, due to pains in her back. She barely made it home.

Due to the location of the pain, the doctors thought perhaps she had kidney stones. Upset and concerned, my parents called their urologist, who was a personal friend. The doctor excused her from school and scheduled a cystoscopy. In September, the procedure was performed. That was the one and only time Helen ever complained. Perhaps she didn't have enough anesthesia, but Helen was miserable in the hospital that night. The doctors found nothing.

Her pain continued. The next step was the pediatrician's office for x-rays and blood work. In October, Helen had an exploratory operation, and doctors found that her lymph nodes were twice the size they should have been. They took a biopsy and placed it in wax. After the surgery, they gave her blood transfusions throughout the night. Dad stayed overnight at the hospital to keep her company.

The next morning, Dad went home to freshen up and get something to eat. When he returned to the hospital, the children's ward was shut down. He couldn't get in. Inside,

Helen was coding. Because of the transfusions, her lungs were filling up with fluid. Once the doctor came out of the room, he relayed the news: "She is fine now, but we almost lost her." Mom and Dad didn't know how they would have dealt with losing her so soon after she initially got sick.

Something was definitely wrong. She was home from the hospital and continued to make frequent trips to the doctor's office, but still, there was no diagnosis.

By the spring of 1967, around Easter time, my parents were frustrated, knowing something was wrong, yet nothing was being done. They wanted a second opinion, so they went to the pediatrician and asked for a recommendation to a well-known hospital in the city. Friends from their church had been to a particular hospital and were pleased with the care and treatment. The doctor told them, "Oh, everyone thinks that place is a mecca," but he had reservations. He recommended another hospital, and he referred them to a physician he knew.

It happened to be a hospital with a religious affiliation, and the nurses were dressed in full habits, which must have been frightening to an eleven-year-old girl. In addition, she went through a battery of unpleasant tests for a week, after which the doctor concluded, "She was faking it." He further suggested my parents "take her home and put her to work." My parents were appalled. They knew Helen was not faking it.

The summer months of 1967 rolled around, and Helen seemed to be feeling a little better. The family decided to go on their summer vacation and drove to Canada to attend the Expo exhibits.

On the trip home, Helen did not feel well. My parents

were still thinking about the other medical center friends had suggested, the so-called mecca the pediatrician had rejected. In August, my mother decided to write a letter to the director of that hospital, explaining Helen's health issues.

In September, they received a reply that they were welcome to bring Helen in for a consultation. On the day of the appointment, a doctor spent the whole afternoon with her. One thing the doctor asked her to do was to push her feet against his hands, and she couldn't do it. She had no strength. The doctor requested all the reports and test results from the other hospital where Helen's original tests and surgery had been completed.

The new doctor and his team of medical colleagues reviewed the original x-rays and the biopsy. In October, they performed surgery, which revealed a malignancy. Finally, they had an answer: it was neuroblastoma, an inoperable tumor that went along the entire length of her spine. The doctor didn't give my parents much hope. My parents said, "We have strong faith. If it is the Lord's will, he will take care of it."

Helen was then referred to an oncologist. Throughout the next year, she was in the hospital for months at a time for chemotherapy and radiation. Helen's solid and unyielding faith kept her spirits high in spite of being away from home. She always had a smile, and her Bible was close by, inspiring the doctors and nurses around her.

My mother was a teacher, and my father worked in the model shop, creating small-scale models, at the local government arsenal. My father said he had a terrific boss who told him whenever he had to leave, he could just go. My parents spent a lot of time traveling since the hospital was an hour away. My grandmother lived with us and always had food ready for them to take on the road. They visited Helen every day she was in the hospital.

Sometimes the trip took longer than the time they were able to stay there. One night, they were detoured, and then the transmission of their car gave them trouble. They finally made it to the hospital after a three-hour trip. Their motto was "Never give up." And they didn't.

There were times when both parents couldn't make the hospital trip. The principal of my mother's school offered to go with her. In addition, there were always friends from their church who wanted to see Helen. They never had to go it alone. People came together to help however they could. Friends made food and sent gifts.

Some of her radiation treatments were done as an outpatient. Part of that procedure was getting blood work ahead of time. On one occasion Dad and Helen were walking down the hall to the elevator, and suddenly, Dad noticed blood running down her arm. She didn't panic; they just turned around and returned to the blood bank, where the staff bandaged her up. She was always agreeable, with a positive attitude and a bright smile.

During the summer of 1968, the family went to a relative's wedding for the weekend. My mother recently found a postcard Helen wrote to a friend on July 12, 1968:

Dear Lily,

How are you? I'm feeling a little better. Last weekend we went to Connecticut instead of going to the shore. We had a lot of fun. We went to my father's cousin's wedding in Ct. It was nice and they were glad to see me. We stayed at a hotel nearby with a pool. We also went to a local park. There we saw animals, went on rides and visited a coal mine. I'm sorry I haven't written sooner but I had to start my sick medicine. So, I'm not feeling my best but when I'm through I will be full of pep. I will write again.

Helen

Unfortunately, the card was never mailed. Six weeks later, on August 16, 1968, Helen lost her fight with cancer.

Almost two years after Helen began to feel ill, she succumbed to the dreadful disease. My parents know they did everything they could possibly have done. Again, their love for each other helped them through the devastating times. Their faith in God never wavered. They know for sure Helen is in heaven. My much younger cousin, whose father had been killed in a tragic car accident a few years earlier, upon hearing the news of Helen's passing, said, "Won't Daddy be happy to see Helen?"

It's been forty-six years, and my parents still think of her every day.

We set up a memorial fund that provided the church with money to buy recording equipment so services and special events can be recorded for those who can't get to church. Cassettes and recorders were lent to people who were sick or shut in. This project continued for ten years, from 1968 to 1978, when a new church was built with updated technology.

Helen's doctor wrote my parents a beautiful handwritten letter they still have today. The doctor said he was Catholic and, as such, was devoted to saints. He truly believed Helen was a saint and someone he'd benefitted from knowing.

The following summer, 1969, my father took us on a month-long vacation to spend time with his family, trying to make up for lost time. We drove from our hometown to Texas to meet up with our cousins. From Texas, we went to the Grand Canyon and Mesa Verde, and we stood in four states at one time at the Four Corners, just to name a few places. It was one of the most memorable family vacations I can recall.

Helen's spirit is still with all of us. I know she has been my guardian angel watching over me with her shining smile.

How do my parents endure? Faith and love.

Smile

Smile when your heart is aching.
Smile even though it's breaking.
When there are clouds in the sky,
you'll get by
if you smile
through your fear and sorrows.
Smile, and maybe tomorrow
you'll see the sun come shining through for you.[1]

Courage isn't having the strength to go on; it is going on when you don't have the strength.

Author unknown

2

DR. TONY, MY HUSBAND

A Story of Strength, Bravery, and Unconditional Love

On our first date, Tony and I closed a local restaurant a few blocks from my apartment in New York. We chatted over coffee and dessert. He was handsome, polite, and smart. As we said good night, he said he would like to see me again. I didn't reveal my excitement.

During our courtship, I asked him why he became a doctor. He jokingly replied, "Because my mother insisted." The truth is, he found the perfect profession. He embodies all that a physician represents: compassion, intelligence, respect, and patience.

As a boy, he grew up in Hoboken, New Jersey. Growing up in an inner-city community during the 1950s and 1960s was difficult since Hoboken was not the gentrified community it is today. At that time, the town was a tough place to live. Since Tony was a bright student, he found the biggest and baddest kid in the school to walk home with him. In return,

Tony did his bodyguard's homework. Tony loved learning and excelled at it, even skipping a grade in school.

Getting into medical school proved problematic for even the smartest student. Accepted to schools outside the United States and being of Italian heritage, Tony set out for Italy. The challenges there were numerous, with the most salient being the language. He could not read, write, or converse in Italian. He had exactly three months to bring up his game before setting out for his final destination to the medical school. For starters, he took a three-month immersion course in Italian language and culture. Then he went on to medical school, where his life in Italian began in earnest. All courses and exams were both written and oral, exclusively in Italian.

To Tony's advantage, many of the students and professors wanted to learn or practice English. Spending time together outside of class was a benefit to all concerned, although there were a few faux pas along the way. One evening, after going to the movies, Tony sat at a café and ordered coffee and a dessert: "Per favore portami un espresso e un canellone." To his surprise, when the order arrived, it was a huge bowl of cannelloni pasta, not the cannoli he'd thought he'd ordered. Too embarrassed to admit his mistake, he proceeded to sit there and eat the main course with gusto.

On another occasion, Tony attended a medical lecture, and at the end, the speaker pointed out there were Americans in the audience. The professor asked Tony in broken English to introduce himself and explain his reason for attending. Tony responded in broken Italian, "Sono inscritto nell primo ano della facolta di medicina." The entire room broke out in laughter, along with the professor. The statement was translated for him: "I'm enrolled in my first asshole of medicine." The key difference between *year* (*anno*) and *asshole* (*ano*) is one letter! It's all in the pronunciation. It was another learning experience among many and the beginning of a wonderful friendship with that professor.

Following the six-year program for his medical degree, Tony returned to the States to continue his studies. He completed three years of internal medicine training and two years of a pulmonary fellowship. Accomplishing all this provided him with the expertise to become a specialist in lung diseases. He went on to the positions of director of pulmonary medicine at a local hospital and medical director of a multispecialty medical group. He loved being a physician. He spent extra time on his training to watch and learn as much as possible. He wanted to be the best, and he became the best. He completed fifteen years of education and training in preparation for his career as a physician.

My husband is a remarkable man and an extremely talented physician. His patients often bring in delicious homemade foods, personalized artwork, and book dedications, and one even wrote a poem for him. Here is an excerpt of that piece, which demonstrates the love his patients have for him:

> Tony is his first name
> Healing is his game
> Nowhere on earth could you find
> A doctor so gentle and kind
> He's loved by everyone he meets
> And especially by the people he treats
> He's never harsh or unkind
> And he also has a brilliant mind.

What happened when this gifted doctor became ill?

The truth is, no one believes an illness will happen to him or her. Yet it doesn't matter who one is or what one does; no one is exempt from life's trials and tribulations.

It started with a pain in his shoulder, which he couldn't explain. A neurologist Tony worked with noticed something wasn't quite right and scheduled an appointment with him. Tony was also sent for a variety of tests, and then he was given the news: he had Parkinson's disease. Wanting to confirm the diagnosis, he visited several renowned medical centers. He was in denial for two years, seeking a diagnosis that was anything but Parkinson's disease.

There are many presentations of Parkinson's, which act differently in each person. In Tony's case, the dystonias (involuntary muscle spasms) were the severest initial symptoms. His body began to play the game Twister without partners. *Twister* was the nickname our family gave to each attack. Tony's arms and legs involuntarily moved into wrap-around positions due to uncontrollable muscle spasms. His arms raised over his head, and there was rotation of the neck and head in one direction or another, in addition to twisting around of the torso and spiraling of the legs. On occasion, I tried to correct his posture by repositioning his arms, but with all my strength, I couldn't move them. To prevent himself from further harm, he would lie on the floor facedown. I would place pillows between his legs and under his shoulders. Sweat fell profusely from his body.

An early morning twister was difficult for our eight-year-old son, David, and me since we did not want to leave Tony on his own. Tony wanted us to continue our daily routine despite his suffering. Luckily, his office manager came to the house every day. Knowing she was always there was comforting to David and me.

Tony continued to work in his office. Few patients were aware of his illness, but on one occasion, during a patient interview with a husband and wife in a relatively small exam room, a twister overcame Tony. He crouched down on the floor between the exam table and the exit door. The patients refused to leave him until the episode passed.

Similar moments occurred infrequently, but the response was always the same: the patients were as concerned for the doctor as the doctor was for them, and they wanted to help him as much as he had helped them through the years.

He took the medications prescribed to him yet found little relief. He read all he could and learned about new studies and findings. One day a colleague told him about a stem-cell program outside the United States that had been featured on a radio station. They harvest one's own stem cells from the crest of the hip bone. Next, the cells are processed. Depending on the viability and quality of the cells, they are then returned to the body by lumbar puncture. The family—Tony, his sister, his nephew, Richie, David, and I—traveled to Germany for the procedure, which was repeated six months later on a second trip. Unfortunately, within the next few years, the program closed due to lack of funding. Consequently, there was not enough research data to know if the therapy was helpful.

Manipulating various medications kept Tony's symptoms at bay, and he defied the initial five-year prognosis before requiring a wheelchair. Then again, he is a fighter.

Suffering for years with severe, painful dystonia, Tony was distraught. The medications were no longer lasting very long, and the dystonia was happening more often. This disorder is very painful, and after many years of enduring the misery, he tearfully said as we lay on the floor to subdue a dystonic episode, "This is not living. I don't know how much more I can take."

A renowned neurologist was recommended to Tony. We met her with great expectation, and she delivered. After several visits, she explained Tony's dystonia was severe, and he would be a great candidate for deep brain stimulation surgery.

This method for treating the symptoms of Parkinson's disease is not a cure, but it improves one's quality of life.

Previously, Tony never had wanted anyone "messing" with his brain. The time had come for Tony to seriously consider this surgery. We researched the DBS procedure, which showed some positive results. We knew someone who had the procedure, so we met with him, and he said, "I would do it again." Following the procedure, he told us, he had been able to do many things he'd been unable to do before, such as ride a bike, drive a car, and pour a glass of wine.

In DBS surgery, two holes are drilled through the skull to admit a pair of titanium wires leading to electrodes that are placed under the skin and attached to pacemaker batteries. Because the patient needs to be awake during the surgery, only local anesthesia is given. The terrifying aspect for Tony was that he would be unable to take the medication he needed to control his symptoms. The doctors would be working in his brain, and he would need to remain still. The solution to the dilemma was that his head would be bolted to a halo device, which would be connected to a CT scanner, keeping the head immobile. As frightening as brain surgery is, taking action against the horror of dystonia empowered all of us, so Tony considered it carefully.

As a physician himself, Tony wanted to know all his options. He consulted with two neurosurgeons at two different hospitals. Typically, the procedure is done in two sessions: the first one is to place the leads on both sides of the brain, and the second is to attach the wires to the batteries. The next doctor he spoke to explained that he did the surgery in three stages to give the brain time to heal between each surgery. That statement resonated with my husband. His instincts told him this doctor was a thinking man, and his option reassured Tony and made him feel comfortable with the doctor's logic.

The day came, and it was time for surgery. Tony was to arrive at the hospital at five thirty in the morning to be prepped, and I was able to stay with him until about eight o'clock in the morning. The first nurse took his temperature, checked his weight, and verified who he was, and he changed into a blue surgical gown. He was then transported to preop, where his head was shaved, an IV was started, and lots of love was sent his way as he was taken to the operating room.

The immediate effects of the first surgery were fantastic. The next day, he walked around the house, saying, "It's so easy to walk; it's not like I'm wading through water." It was a glimpse of what the future held, giving Tony renewed hope.

It has been several years since the surgery, and Tony has not had any dystonia since then. Thank you, God, and thank you, doctors!

Tony now enjoys an improved quality of life. The surgery was completed in March 2013. Friends and family walked that year in the Parkinson Unity Walk through a park, while Tony rode his bike along the course. It was a fantastic day! For our next adventure, the family celebrated by going on vacation together for the first time in ten years. Perhaps Tony will even get to visit Italy again.

Tony continues to work in his office. He lives on to help others. How did Tony endure? Love, determination, and hope.

Here Comes the Sun

Little darling, it's been a long, cold, lonely winter.
Little darling, it feels like years since it's been here
Here comes the sun; here comes the sun,
and I say it's all right.
Little darling, the smiles returning to the faces.
Little darling, it seems like years since it's been here.[2]

When you can't find the sunshine,
be the sunshine.

Ed Lester

3

RICHIE, MY STEPSON

A Story of Love, Dedication, and Passion

After several months of dating Tony, I met his adorable son, Richie, who was eight years old at the time. I was more concerned about meeting him than any other family member. If Richie didn't approve, I was a goner. Luckily, we got along and enjoyed each other's company. Richie's mother once told me Richie knew his father and I would get married before I knew.

Richie was ten years old when his dad and I married. His skills at speaking and singing were evident at our wedding as he delivered a toast to his dad, making everyone laugh, and then he finished by singing "Wind beneath My Wings," bringing everyone to tears.

Richie lives an extraordinary life and lives it fully. In elementary school, Richie found his passion by playing his first acting role as a charismatic character in *Bye Bye Birdie* while dressed in a gold lamé suit. Throughout his middle school and high school years, he excelled in many theatrical presentations.

Richie is highly intelligent and graduated from college magna cum laude with a triple major in biology, theater, and dance. Career-wise, he could have taken the easy path, entering into the successful family business started by his grandfather, but that is not the way his family works. They are motivated self-starters with endless energy and talent.

Fresh out of college, Richie auditioned for numerous Broadway shows. He loved the theater. Months went by with no results. He began thinking perhaps he should take the MCAT exam and go to medical school, when suddenly, he had a callback, and then he began living his dream on Broadway. Singing, acting, and dancing became his daily routine, yet it was not enough to completely satisfy him; hence, he answered another call, an internal call to help others. He learned of an organization affiliated with the theater that traveled to South Africa to work with children in need. The children selected to attend the unique experience learned a dance routine during their week at the camp. Richie saw firsthand the life those children endured.

A friend wrote a song for Richie demonstrating how this charitable work was an inspiration not only to the children but also to Richie. Here is an excerpt:

> I never wanted for anything. I didn't cuz I had everything …
>
> And so I took a trip

to see some kids,
to perform …

where I had the privilege
of teaching and working with
some of the most remarkable children,

and I will never forget for my entire life,
and I will always remember

little Septemba, seven years old,
who would take some of the chicken
we provided for lunches every day,
like a quarter of a chicken,
and she would eat a little bit of it, and
she would wrap the rest up and stick it in her
"Broadway in South Africa" shirt, and
she would take it home to share with her
family every single day.

And that, that changed my life.

Children so young
performed what they never knew.

They were living in shacks
and eating rice without spoons.

And on the other side of the hill,
the wealthy all stood still.
And I thought,

Strange.

On Richie's return trip home, he was aware he had been bitten on his knee by a spider. His knee began swelling up on the flight home. The wound festered and was a major threat to his life and limb. He was advised to get off the plane and seek immediate medical attention. Richie explained he was in the middle of nowhere and would seek help when he got home. His family met him at the airport, from which he went directly to the hospital, where he was on IV medication for four days.

That experience didn't stop Richie from returning to Africa. On another trip, he visited Malawi with an organization whose goal was to break the cycle of poverty, illiteracy, and low expectations through service and education. Groups of volunteers joined together with communities throughout the world to build schools. It was a labor of love. In Africa, there was no running water. At the well, once water was pumped, a little bleach was added to purify it, and then it was boiled. Richie learned how incredibly lucky we are to live in this amazing country of the United States of America. In February 2014, this organization honored Richie with the Humanitarian Award.

Richie's fantastic life was not immune to challenges. Perhaps his trip to Africa was his running away from reality. He was involved in a toxic affair and needed space. Relationships are complicated, yet ones that are all-consuming and codependent are not based on trust, honesty, or love. We all want a special someone, yet a relationship filled with lies and deceit is destined for disaster. Toxic relationships are not love. Everyone deserves respect.

Richie has learned not to take anything for granted. My aunt once said upon meeting Richie when he was a child, "He never meets a stranger." He overflows with his exuberant spirit. He treats others with respect and dignity. His mantra is "Shine bright like a Richie."

As a proud, compassionate, talented gay man, Richie believes in being true to oneself. His coming-out journey was short but poignant. Looking back, he believes the reason it took him a while to come out was because, having grown up in a small town, he had no openly gay people to look up to. College is a time when many young people begin to learn and understand more of who they are. At twenty-one, after his college experience, Richie came out to his family. Due to his Italian roots, it took his family a few months to fully accept this reality. Richie credits his grandpa with asking everyone, "Do we all love Richie unconditionally?" Everyone did, so Grandpa added, "We have to stop with conditions." His grandfather then bellowed in the kitchen one afternoon, "What are we going to do—love him any less?" and that was the end of the discussion.

Richie now spreads his message on social media sites and on his blog: "Shine bright."

In today's world, violence and anger get the majority of publicity. When Richie says, "Shine bright," he wants people to be happy with themselves and not allow the misery of someone else to cloud their cheerfulness. When people throw shade, eliciting darkness, overwhelm them with kindness, and do not be discouraged.

Richie wasn't bullied about being gay until his presence on social media. Once he started to have millions of followers, he was exposed to the entire world and not just the liberal cities in which he lives. He was shocked. The bullying and hatred were astounding! The responses to his social media postings include comments such as "You shouldn't have been born," "You don't have the right to live," and "I hate queers." It took Richie years to figure out how to deal with the negativity. He prays for the haters to get better. Hatred is not good for the soul.

Hatred hurts. The negativity caused Richie to drown himself in alcohol. He also had trouble sleeping, and he was prescribed pills to help him sleep and then pills to wake up. The hatred took its toll. Richie sought help from family and friends. He gave up alcohol and pills and has been sober for almost three years.

As I said, Richie's mantra is "Shine bright like a Richie," and when people throw shade, shine brighter! He has been a target of hate. When that happens, be more of your loving self. He explains, "All of you are beautiful and perfect as long as you are being true to yourself and what brings you happiness. That may mean wearing glitter as an outward personification of your inner self or owning your gender or sexuality regardless of the social restraints society has set in place as an obstacle." Most importantly, Richie believes everyone should be who he or she is. "If others can't handle it, it's their problem, not yours." When one fights hate with love, love wins.

Thank you, Richie, for bringing hope to others and being a conduit for peace and love.

How does Richie endure? Love, charity, passion, and shining brighter every day!

Diamonds

Shine bright like a diamond.
Find light in the beautiful sea.
I choose to be happy.
You and I, you and I, we're like diamonds in the sky.
You're a shooting star I see, a vision of ecstasy.
When you hold me, I'm alive. We're like diamonds in the sky.[3]

FRIENDS

This book became a reality because of a seminar I attended recommended by Sifu, the headmaster of a kung fu academy.

The remarkable journeys of all of the following people, recounted firsthand or in interviews with me, demonstrate how having faith, being optimistic and hopeful, and having a dream can be achieved against all odds.

Once you choose hope, anything's possible.

Christopher Reeve

4

SIFU KEITH

A Story of Determination, Passion, and Faith

Keith loved martial arts. As a ten-year-old, he began training at the YMCA in his Long Island community. His instructor guided and educated Keith in kung fu for fourteen years. He was so skilled that as a high school freshman going out for wrestling, he was put on the varsity team. Kung fu prepared him with unbelievable talents, and he loved it. In his senior year, he wrote in his yearbook that he was going to be a world champion by the time he was twenty-two years old. It was a brave and bold statement. It also meant he was going to spend his time training and not going to college. He had to break the news to his parents.

Keith's parents had moved from the Bahamas to the United States to afford their children more opportunities. They worked hard to provide for the family, encountering many challenges, including learning a new language and finding the right neighborhood to live in. Today Keith's daughter laughs at his stories about the places where he used to live and the types of difficulties he had to overcome. She knows nothing about hardships yet, and he tells her these stories in an effort to help her understand that nothing should be taken for granted.

Like many parents, Keith's wanted their children to choose college career paths leading to responsible professions as doctors, lawyers, or engineers. Keith excelled in school, and early in his senior year of high school, he was planning to go to college to study art. However, when going to take the art exam, he looked around and thought, *I don't belong here. This doesn't fit me, and this is not who I am.* He asked himself, *What is it I really want to do?*

Unwilling to accede to Keith's wishes, his parents tried to entice him to continue his education. They brought a steady stream of people over to the house to meet and speak with him about the value of a college degree. He finally had to be brutally honest and say, "I understand the consequences of my actions, and I accept responsibility for them." His dad was also clear: if Keith went to college, they would help him out financially; if he didn't, he was on his own. Keith understood.

After graduating from high school, Keith worked all summer to save money. He then bought a one-way ticket to travel across the country to train in kung fu. It was the first time a family member had left home. His parents thought he'd lost his mind, but Keith remained determined. He knew his father had been on his own since he was sixteen; therefore, he could do this. Keith didn't fear anything or anyone. He was steadfast in knowing that was what he was meant to do.

Keith had made plans to train with two of the top martial artists, Eric Chen and Keith Hirabayashi. He had the incredible opportunity to work with one of the all-time-greatest martial arts forms competitors and one of the most knowledgeable Chinese martial artists in wushu, a contemporary form of Chinese martial arts that emphasizes quickness, power, and natural, relaxed movements.

Keith trained all day every single day. They started their workouts on the beach every morning. Afternoons included intense private lessons that focused on perfecting Keith's form. Next, he practiced with weapons. The evenings began at 7:30 p.m. with a rigorous group session that lasted until 11:30 p.m. He was ready and willing to work hard, and he was relentless.

Keith's funds supported him for about one month. He returned home to work and raise money. His time spent out of state was short yet a phenomenal and tremendous learning experience. Friends who saw him on his return remarked that he'd progressed in strength and technical ability by three years' worth of training instead of a few weeks.

Upon returning home, he accepted various jobs that were flexible and permitted him to continue his training. He taught martial arts both privately and at a karate school. Being allowed to teach kung fu at a karate school was a privilege, and accordingly, he was asked to study the karate martial arts system. As a result, he earned a second-degree black belt in karate.

Keeping his expenses down, he used public transportation or walked, which gave him the freedom to choose what he wanted to do and not be burdened financially. Determined in his pursuit of martial arts experiences and training, he finally purchased a car to travel for competitions. Interestingly, Keith says martial arts always led him to the next thing. He got a job as a manager of a video store, which allowed him to travel.

The world championship tournaments were held every two years in the 1980s and 1990s. Keith graduated from high school in 1986 and went cross-country that fall. In 1987, his trainer won the world championship. He continued to be inspired and encouraged in his quest to achieve his dream. Then everything changed.

When Keith was driving home from work one day, a car came speeding out of nowhere and cut in front of him. He slammed on the brakes, and his own car spun out of control, crossing over several lanes of traffic. Luckily, no one was in the other lanes. Keith felt dazed and disoriented as he slowly made his way to the side of the road and stopped his car. Then he experienced pain in his neck as he tried to move his head. He sat there for what seemed hours, trying to understand what had just happened. No one stopped, and the police did not come. The other driver continued on, never knowing the damage he or she had caused with his or her reckless driving.

Keith went to the emergency room, had x-rays taken, and was told he had a nerve impingement. One wrong move could leave him paralyzed. The doctor then spoke the most dreaded words Keith could have heard: "No more kung fu."

Devastated doesn't begin to describe how he felt. In an instant, his dream of being a world champion was gone. God had spared his life, but now what?

Being true to oneself and one's passion is not always an easy path.

As a result of his upbringing, he was not afraid of hard work. He had grown up believing that one had to work hard for what one had. He realized, though, that if one were going to succeed and invest many hours in doing something, it might as well be something one enjoyed. In addition, when one was young and idealistic, passion took precedence over making money.

For years, people had told Keith he needed a plan B, but he had been adamant: "No, no, no, I don't need a plan B. I'll be all right." Suddenly, he was faced with a new situation, and he had no plan B. He couldn't pursue what he loved and wanted to do. Maybe everyone else had been right and he had been wrong. It was an emotionally and mentally challenging time, in addition to the pain of his physical injuries.

The following year, Keith went to tournaments as a spectator, watching other people win competitions he knew he could have won, because he had won against those competitors before. It was torture and terribly depressing.

He started to hang out with people with questionable reputations. There were days when he stayed in bed all day and nights when he partied all night.

He felt lost and no longer knew what he wanted, what to do, or who he was.

He realized, *This is not the life I want to lead*, and he asked himself, *What am I going to do from here?* Keith had heard from many people who'd given up things in their lives, and he never wanted to be that person.

One day he had an in-depth conversation with his cousin Paul about life and athletics, and Keith said to him, "You know, I really want to come back. I only have this life, and I might as well live it." He had no plan B.

But the doctors said, "No martial arts." Competing in tournaments includes various forms, acrobatics, fighting, and weapons at the highest level of performance. That was going to be extremely difficult and dangerous, given Keith's injuries. In spite of that, he decided he would come back. He made a conscious decision to concentrate on forms of his practice in which he performed a specific set of movements in a specific sequence, giving up the actual fighting.

His family members were concerned about the consequences of his decision. Loved ones are typically going to be on the side of caution and want one to play it safe, keeping one's best interest at heart.

Somewhere in Keith's heart, he felt there was much more he could achieve. He decided whatever the consequences were, he was going to take responsibility for the life he had and be determined enough to say, "This is what I really want. I'm going to make my dreams come true."

Keith was smart about his return to martial arts. He began working with Ron, a trainer who went on to become a six-time world champion. Ron was blind in one eye and had overcome numerous injuries. Working with him was great for Keith because Ron understood where he was coming from. Limitation is limitation. This was about one's passion and doing one's best, which was how Ron lived.

Keith had stated in his high school yearbook that he would be a world champion by the age of twenty-two. His dream had been temporarily interrupted, but with perseverance and determination, Keith became a world champion in 1990, just a few months after his twenty-second birthday.

Today Keith's academy embodies his "Yes, I can" attitude.

It is a place that inspires the students to do their best and a place of hope in knowing their lives can be whatever they want them to be. In obstacles, there are opportunities. The Chinese word for *crisis* has the word *opportunity* in the character. In everything Keith does, everything he touches, there is an element of optimistic belief. He says if he can help more people have that, then he has lived his purpose.

To Keith, the martial arts are a metaphor for life: "When you look at martial arts training, the person you must overcome is not the opponent; it's yourself. It's your thinking, your discipline, your perseverance, and your self-confidence all staring you in the mirror in the most real way they can."

Once, in Keith's early years of training, his instructor was teaching the students how to break boards, and it was getting easy, so they got cocky. The instructor brought out a brick, and suddenly, the students weren't as self-assured anymore. His instructor said, "It's about going to the next level and how you mentally prepare to do that. The day I decided I was going through the brick is the day I actually did." Keith believes life is a lot like that, and that's what one learns from martial arts.

Keith's story isn't complete without mentioning his faith. God is very important to him, and his belief in God is the foundation of all he does. He recently had the opportunity to speak with the CEO of a large company. Keith asked this impressive man how he got through the difficult times, and the CEO responded that he leaned on God, not to solve his problems but to give him the strength to get through them. Keith agrees with the prayer "Give me the strength to get through this."

We all learn from those around us. Keith credits his dad with being his greatest influence outside of martial arts. He always admired his dad's strength and determination to accomplish his goals. Keith's ultimate goal is to pass on that strength and determination to his children. Like father like son.

Keith's achievements have been featured on television and radio shows throughout the country. He blogs for news publications and is the author of four books.

When asked to discuss the people and activities he is involved with in the entertainment world, he exposes his humble nature: "It's not really about all the entertainment stuff I do; it's more about constantly stretching yourself and continuing to grow as a person. If someone had told me when I was a teen that I would be doing half the things I've done or am doing, I would have said, 'No way.' I can remember walking into the offices of a National Football League team as an off-season training coach and thinking, *What! Pinching me!* or waiting in the green room to go on a popular daytime talk show and thinking, *This is amazing!*"

Keith continues to spread positive, inspiring messages. He is the consummate instructor in martial arts and the art of living. In April 2015, he sponsored his first seminar focusing on finding balance in one's life. It was a fantastic weekend in the mountains that encouraged people to live their best life. The overall theme was "Mind, body, and spirit." The day began by waking up the body with tai chi; the mind and body were nourished with deliciously prepared, fresh local foods under the guidance of a nutritionist; and the mind and spirit were engaged during fascinating discussions.

How does Keith endure? Determination, faith, and love.

The Impossible Dream

To dream the impossible dream.
To fight the unbearable foe.
To bear with unbearable sorrow.
To run where the brave dare not go.
To right the unrightable wrong.
To love pure and chaste from afar.
To try when your arms are too weary.
To reach the unreachable star.[4]

You do not need to know precisely what is happening, or exactly where it is all going. What you need is to recognize the possibilities and challenges offered by the present moment and embrace them with courage, faith and hope.

Thomas Merton

5

RON AND LAURA

A Story of Love and Compassion

Early in their journey together, Laura remembers her husband, Ron, saying, "Martial arts saved my life."

As a child growing up in severe poverty, Ron was the youngest of seven children, and his father left when he was born. Ron's mother was on welfare and worked two jobs in Chelsea, a town with a high crime rate, known as the City of Sin. It was a rough and tough place to grow up.

Ron was small for his age, which, especially in Chelsea, made being teased a regular occurrence. He was playing in a vacant lot one day and found a shard of glass, which he used to strip leaves from a branch. A piece of the glass broke off and flew into his eye, causing him to lose the vision in that eye. The patch he wore after that gave kids another reason to ridicule him.

When he was ten, Ron discovered martial arts, which saved his life in more ways than one. As he got older, it gave him focus, direction, and self-confidence. He always had ambition, which reinforced his passion for martial arts.

Ron met a sensei, a karate master. As a young boy, he loved Bruce Lee movies and the 1970s David Carradine show *Kung Fu*, and the martial arts training made him feel alive. He now had something to put his energy and focus toward. Studying with this sensei was a dream come true.

The sensei was like a father figure for Ron. The studio gave him a place to go, allowing him to stay off the streets and out of trouble—not an easy thing to do in his town. Trouble was everywhere.

As a child, Ron had a talent for drawing. He used his artistic ability to create murals and design logos in exchange for his martial arts classes when he couldn't afford to pay for lessons.

After achieving his first black belt in karate at age thirteen, he switched to the martial art of kung fu. This style was more flexible, allowing flips, high kicks, and the use of weapons.

Energetic and focused, as a teen of fourteen, he was up at dawn, practicing outside before the studio opened. Once the studio was open, Ron attended classes and trained all day.

After training with his first sensei, he trained in kung fu and became a kung fu expert. In his later years, he worked with world-famous coaches, who later said with intense admiration that Ron embodied everything a true martial artist stood for.

Ron started winning tournaments locally, regionally, and state-wide. He was such a strong competitor that if other athletes knew he was competing, they wouldn't even sign up! He got yelled at: "You're ruining the tournament for everyone!" He was told he should go to the West Coast to compete. That meant he was ready for the national level.

After becoming the first person in his family to graduate from high school, Ron continued to train while working to support his family. He incorporated kung fu into every task. As he buffed cars, he put his heart and soul into that manual-labor job to build up his strength. Wax on, wax off.

Working at the local airport, he would stand in horse stance. This common posture in Asian martial arts is a position assumed when riding a horse. First, you stand straight with legs apart and feet facing forward. Next, bend the knees, and lower the upper body as if sitting on horseback. Then shift the body and weight forward into a forward stance. As Ron stood in horse stance, he would pick up a piece of luggage in each hand, move to a forward stance, drop the bags, go back to the original horse-stance position, and repeat. The job provided the money that allowed Ron to travel to competitions held in other parts of the country.

As a young man, he had been dating a woman for a short time, when they discovered she was pregnant. To Ron, there was no question of what to do. Wanting to do the "right thing," he felt there was only one decision: marriage. A few years later, another child was born. His dedication and commitment to martial arts were a way to provide a better life for his children. They always had his unconditional love.

Ron was a champion within his chosen discipline, but he also was accomplished in everything he did. His entire life revolved around discipline, determination, perseverance, passion, and love. He was a man of remarkable talent and ability. These attributes didn't protect him from marital challenges. When his marriage ended, he moved across the country to the West Coast as a single father with his two sons.

Ron worked in a number of jobs and was an original stunt cast member of a popular superhero television show. He was a real-life superhero. He was also on a live-action television show featuring martial artists and continued to train and teach.

One day Laura walked into his life. One of her coworkers had invited her to attend an exercise class at the gym where Ron taught. Laura was a twenty-six-year-old workaholic at a design agency, trying to climb the corporate ladder. Going to the class meant leaving work at five o'clock in the afternoon. She wondered, *Who does that?*

But she went to the studio and took the class, which turned out to be an incredible workout. She attended a few more times and soon joined the gym.

On Saturday mornings, in making an 8:45 a.m. class after working all week, Laura was proud of herself, even though she typically rushed in without makeup and in a baggy sweatshirt.

That was not the typical attire of women at the studio. Laura wondered how they all managed to look so gorgeous after a strenuous workout. Out of the corner of her eye, she watched the beautiful women fawn all over the instructor, a guy named Ron. Before class, they would ask if they could help get the music ready, and after class, they commented on how terrific the lesson had been. Someone brought him coffee, and another woman offered him a blueberry muffin. Everyone was genuine with their admiration, but Laura wondered what the big deal was with the guy.

One particular Saturday, Laura decided to take two classes. During the five-minute break between the classes,

Ron noticed she had signed up to take two lessons. Seemingly impressed, he commented on her taking two classes, to which she responded, "I'm going to try." Continuing the conversation, Laura asked if there were any Pilates studios opening up. They were becoming popular at the time, and she had a background in dance and ballet. She thought the gym would know what was happening in the neighborhood, particularly in terms of fitness.

Ron had never heard of Pilates and asked, "What's that?"

After Laura explained Pilates to him, he thought it sounded like the style of martial arts he practiced, wushu, and suggested she should come try a class.

"Oh no, thank you," she replied. He then mentioned private lessons for personal training. Thinking to herself that she didn't need someone yelling at her to exercise and that it was not in her budget anyway, she kindly replied,

"No, but thank you."

Ron said, "Because you're a member of the studio, the first lesson is free."

How could she say no to free? Laura took the free lesson, stayed with the classes, and enjoyed them without really knowing anything more about Ron.

Typically, their lessons were late in the evening, after the group classes had finished. Ron would stay late to work with her. One evening, Laura commented on how hungry she was, and Ron replied, "Let's get something to eat." That was their first time out together. Afterward, they continued to spend more and more time with each other.

Word was getting around. Laura's coworker asked, "Hey, what's going on with you and Ron?"

Laura said, "Nothing. It's not a big deal."

Her coworker told her how much all the women at the gym loved him and said, "He's the most eligible bachelor in that little world."

Laura said, "I just don't get it."

The coworker proceeded to explain all of Ron's achievements and awards. In all the time he and Laura spent together, he was humble and never spoke of himself.

After three months of dating, Ron said to Laura, "I'm going to marry you." She told him he was crazy, but Ron insisted he was going to marry her one day.

As time went on, their relationship progressed, and their bond grew even stronger. Laura decided to take a break from her stressful position at the design agency, which allowed them to spend more time together, and their relationship grew stronger.

Together they opened up a studio, which solidified their powerful bond.

As Laura related the story of her life with Ron to me, she said he faced numerous formidable situations over the years, and at the end of the day, he was never bitter and never made excuses for why he wasn't somewhere in his career or doing something based on circumstances. He always tried to do better for himself and his family.

Laura was ten years younger than he, and at first, she didn't realize he had children. When she found out, it was a huge decision for her to consciously continue the relationship.

She saw a man who was always affectionate with his boys, as they were with him. There was something special about a man who was so loving and sweet with his children.

She saw and felt the love.

After being together for almost six years, Ron and Laura got married on July 1, 2006. They had two children. Laura was up with their daughter every two hours. Ron would get up just to sit with her, help with diaper changes, and keep her company in spite of the need to go to work early the next day. When their son was born prematurely, Ron's love and devotion overflowed even more as their family grew.

Ron was Laura's husband, but first and foremost, he was her best friend.

Without any warning, in May 2013, Ron was diagnosed with stage-four pancreatic cancer. Most people who knew Ron believed that if anyone could beat that devastating disease, it was him.

He continued to go to the studio despite the exhaustion, excruciating pain, and Laura's pleas for him to rest. Per Ron's wishes, they kept details of his illness a private matter, as he was always considerate and did not want to burden others with the news. He was fiercely protective of his family, and he did not want cancer to take over his identity and become the lens people saw him through or define how people related to him. They were hopeful the new medications would be the healing treatment. It was not meant to be.

In December 2013, seven months after his diagnosis, Ron lost his battle to this dreadful disease. Life continued for Laura and their two children.

Ron lived his life fully. He never had intended to get married again. He had been down and disenchanted. Then he'd met his angel, Laura.

Many people considered Ron a superhero able to do

the impossible. In my opinion, Laura was Ron's hero, and she continues to carry on his legacy.

Her reality is caring for their children, taking them to school, making lunches, and potty-training their two-year-old son, who is about to begin preschool. To support their family, she has two jobs in addition to running the studio.

How does Laura endure? Love.

Hero

There's a hero
if you look inside your heart.
You don't have to be afraid
of what you are.
There's an answer
if you reach into your soul.
And the sorrow that you know
will melt away.[5]

Yesterday is but a dream. Tomorrow is only a vision. But today well lived makes every yesterday a dream of happiness, and every tomorrow a vision of hope.

Kalidasa, *The Complete Works of Kalidasa*

6

ANNA

A Story of Perseverance, Determination, and Love

When I attended Anna's seminar in Philadelphia, I never expected to learn the full story behind this extraordinary person. I went to be a supportive participant and to better understand her remarkable organization, Melanie's Boot Camp, which she founded to help women break the cycle of domestic violence.

The day began with the guests playing a few games to get to know each other in a fun, friendly atmosphere. Anna then started the seminar by telling the story of her life.

When she was five years old, Anna stood on the sidewalk between Broad and Market Streets in Philadelphia and felt her world crumble when she watched her stepfather hit her mother. It was just the beginning of a nightmare of abuse.

Anna felt it was a bizarre paradox since they went to church all the time, yet she lived in a den of horror, physical abuse, and sexual tension.

Four years later, when Anna was nine years old, her stepfather moved the family to the Dominican Republic. The relocation removed her mother from the support system of her family, including her brother, who lived close by, and her friends, along with the familiar city in which she had lived her entire life.

Anna moved from the vibrant, active world of Philadelphia to the mountains of the Dominican Republic, where there were farm animals roaming around and the closest house was about a mile away. In addition, she didn't speak the language in the new country, so she didn't attend school for her first year there. But Anna was resilient. She learned the language and adapted to her new culture and the rural life, climbing trees and picking fruit. After five years, that became her home.

Unfortunately, the violence continued. Anna often left the house and roamed the streets in an effort to leave the hurtfulness behind. In the middle of one night, after hearing her mother's screams, she ran to a neighbor's house and banged on the door. After that, she blacked out. Blackouts are losses of memory that sometimes develop after people experience trauma. Anna doesn't remember the details but believes the police were called, and the crisis was resolved.

When the abuse turned toward Anna, her mother fought back, kicking her stepfather out of the house. He was finally gone. Her mother began making up for lost time. Instead of Anna and her siblings being sent away to a relative's house during the holidays, the family stayed together. Life was getting better.

At fourteen, Anna went on vacation to visit her uncle in Philadelphia. One night, the phone rang, and the call delivered news that would again change her life: her mother had been killed in a car accident. Her three-year-old little brother had run into a busy street, and as her mother had run after him and pushed him out of the way to save him, she had been struck and killed by an oncoming truck.

Anna never went back to the Dominican Republic. She had no closure and no chance to say a final goodbye. The agony and pain of losing a family member is heartbreaking and, under such circumstances, unfathomable. She lost her mom, her home, her school, her friends, and her whole life, including her two little brothers, who went into foster care. She didn't see them for about two years.

How did Anna cope? She became a rebellious teen involved with sex, drugs, and hip-hop in the 1980s. She got pregnant at nineteen; moved in with her boyfriend; and, months later, delivered her precious twin boys.

Being thrust into adulthood was not easy. The challenges were endless, and the babies added continual obligations. In addition, the other grown-up in the household was demanding and needy. Suddenly, when she didn't respond to one of her boyfriend's needs, he hit her so hard she fell to the floor. Caught off guard and trembling, she realized what scared her the most was seeing the fear in her sons' eyes. In that moment, she made the decision to pack up her boys and leave, putting an end to the cycle of domestic violence in her family.

Anna trained to become an EMT and went to work for the fire department in emergency medical services, operations, and communications. She worked on the streets of Philadelphia, helping people, for seventeen years.

She has seen everything. She has delivered babies, she has had brains and livers in her hands, and she has had intestines and you-name-it splattered all over her. Anna says her career has been an amazing gift to make her the person she is today.

In contrast, the stress of her birth-family environment left its mark on her siblings, with one brother being institutionalized and another being incarcerated.

Anna strived to make sense of all the adversity in her personal life. For twenty years, she sought answers through personal development and research. She has gotten through many stages of healing and accepted the realization that people she encountered played out the roles they felt they needed to play out. Her stepfather played his role of the abuser, and her mom played her role as the abused. They were unconscious and automatic roles. Anna feels she is not one to judge them, because they were in their own process, their own evolution.

Anna's birth family was very religious. When her mom died, Anna ran away from religion and God. Over the past five years of working through life's challenges with the assistance of a life coach and reading numerous books, she has come back to God, allowing him back into her heart and life. Prior, she was angry, judgmental, and cynical about religion.

In honor of her mother, Anna has created an organization to help women living in domestic-violence environments: Melanie's Boot Camp. Anna works tirelessly to bring women together, providing personal-growth and development seminars for survivors of abuse. Her goal is to empower people and shift their mentality from victim to victor.

I asked Anna who her hero is. She paused for a moment

and then responded, "I am my hero."

One of her favorite moments at the boot camp she sponsors ever year is when she stands in front of a roomful of women and says, "I'm friggin' awesome!" Inevitably, they look at her as if to say, *Okay?* and then she says, "And you know what? You're friggin' awesome too!"

Anna hated herself for forty years, engaging in self-loathing for most of her life. For her to acknowledge "I am my hero" is an amazing accomplishment.

How does Anna endure? Strength, determination, faith, and love.

When You Believe

There can be miracles
when you believe.
Though hope is frail,
it's hard to kill.

Who knows what miracles
you can achieve
when you believe somehow you will?

You will when you believe.[6]

Hope is not the closing of your eyes to the difficulty, the risk, or the failure.

It is a trust—if I fail now, I shall not fail forever; and if I am hurt, I shall be healed.

It is a trust that life is good, love is powerful, and the future is full of promise.

Author unknown

7

SALLY

A Story of Triumph against All Odds

Turmoil surrounded Sally for the first four years of her life. Her mother, Mary, was married at fifteen, and shortly after the birth of her youngest daughter, Sally, her husband brought another woman he was going to marry into their home. It was acceptable to have more than one wife in the Egyptian Muslim culture, but after fourteen years of marriage, Mary's husband ordered Mary to leave and divorced her. Mary went back to her childhood home, looking for solace, but with her stepmother in charge, Mary and her children were not welcome. In spite of the hostile greeting, she stayed there with her children for about one and a half years.

Mary's sister needed help with her children, which led to an opportunity to go to France to become their nanny. Mary took the offer, but unfortunately, Sally's father refused to allow Sally's three older siblings to travel with Sally and her mother, creating more heartache for Mary.

Life in France was not what Mary expected. A friend

of her brother-in-law liked Mary and wanted to marry her. Even though she was not in love with the man, Omar, she believed a marriage to him would allow her to stay in France and have a good life for herself and Sally. Alas, Omar was an alcoholic with abusive tendencies.

One night, he came home intoxicated and put a knife to Mary's throat, saying he was going to kill her. Luckily, he granted her one last wish to say farewell to Sally and her baby sister. Mary, sobbing, ran upstairs and realized Omar had stopped pursuing her. She tiptoed back down the stairs to find him passed out cold.

Mary took Sally and her four-month-old baby sister to live in a women's shelter. Once they were on their own, Mary had to learn French and go to work to support herself and her daughters. The environment was not the greatest in which to raise a family. The shelter was filled with drug addicts and women of the night. Nonetheless, they were befriended by a woman and her young daughter who'd escaped the genocide in Africa. This was in 1987.

Mary worked cleaning houses, picking potatoes, and doing whatever she could to earn money. After a few years, they moved to another shelter, where they lived in a studio apartment. Even though Sally was only seven years old, she needed to take on more responsibility. She picked up her younger sister after school and, once home, had chores to do: cleaning up the apartment, cooking, and doing the dishes. Since Mary didn't read or write in French, Sally read the bills that came in and filled out the forms for packages being sent to Egypt for Mary's other children. Sally's mother's sole purpose in life was to get her children back from her first marriage. She was always fighting for her kids.

For Sally, starting school in Europe proved to be challenging. The students in their Caucasian French community were nasty to her. She never realized she was different until the kids called her names, including Big Nose and Unibrow. One boy would trip her, causing her to fall, every day, over and over again. Finally, Sally had had enough and hit him in the face. Of course, that got her into trouble, but the boy never tripped her again.

She faced constant racism, even from some of her teachers. One teacher continually pulled Sally's full, curly hair, bringing tears to her eyes. Sally just wanted to fit in, always trying to figure out her place in the world. Sally desperately wanted to talk to her mom about life, but Mary wasn't emotionally available.

Poverty played a huge role in Sally's life. From the ages of six to twelve, she and her sister went to visit a foster family on weekends. The foster family treated them well, taking them to the theater and horseback riding. They lived in the country, in a big house that allowed the two sisters the exciting experience of having their own rooms. Confusion arose when the French couple bathed and showered together with the girls. The couple were very open, yet at age twelve, Sally was not accustomed to seeing a grown man and woman naked. She felt uncomfortable and refused to go back to visit.

Sally's teenage years were filled with confusion about religion and culture. Writing in her journal, she wondered why she had to be covered up and couldn't wear makeup, and dating was out of the question. The girls in France could have long hair, and it wasn't a big deal to wear miniskirts and makeup. Mary was strict with her daughters because that was all she knew.

In order to do things that felt more normal to her, Sally began lying to her mom. She did not lie so she could go out drinking, which didn't interest her, but she wanted the freedom to go to the big city or stay at a friend's house.

Sally's entrepreneurial aptitude emerged at a young age. She would collect items from neighbors and then sell them at the Sunday market. In school, she asked if she could do any work at the school during the long lunch break. She began weeding the schoolyard, doing dishes in the cafeteria, and doing whatever else needed to be done. She was given about fifteen dollars a month, which was like gold to her.

Getting older and hating school, Sally found another way to earn money. Stealing items and reselling them made it possible for her to purchase a pair of Levi's jeans she desired. One day a plainclothes security person tapped her on the shoulder and said, "Follow me."

Sally put up a fight but eventually surrendered the stolen items. Suddenly, something changed. To Sally, the officer was an older man who she believed could see her pain. She wanted to be tough; she didn't want him to see her cry. After his lecture, he put a hand out to shake, saying, "I will let you go this time, but don't ever come back here." As Sally went to shake his hand, he embraced her in a warm, kind hug. She felt an angel had come into her life to give her a message, perhaps changing the path she eventually took in her life.

Always wanting her freedom, she planned to move from the village of Croix-Rouge, France, to a larger city after she graduated from high school. Knowing her mother would never let her move on her own, Sally waited until Mary traveled to Egypt for the summer. As soon as her mother left, Sally applied for a job in the city and was hired at a fast-food restaurant. Next, she started her search for an apartment and found a studio in the perfect neighborhood for her job. She felt freedom for the first time in her life and enjoyed every moment of it. She didn't even mind that she slept on the floor and didn't have any furniture. She was finally free!

Then her mother came back from Egypt. When Mary found out Sally had moved to the city and had her own apartment, she was furious. There was a huge fight, which led to a year of not speaking to each other. A religious girl did not leave the house until she was married, but Sally didn't care.

The next three years of living on her own proved to be a great learning experience in many ways for Sally. She met her first boyfriend and fell in love. He treated her well, yet not having any dating experience, she missed certain signs that all might not have been well with him. For example, they always went to her apartment for dinner and to hang out, and she never saw him on weekends.

One day a friend said to her, "You know he is married, don't you?" She'd had no idea. She hadn't realized people cheated.

Success was a personal goal to Sally; she always had wanted to do something big. She loved living in the city yet wanted to go farther away. She wanted to go to America. She didn't know how or when, but she put her thoughts out into the universe.

One day, while taking a bus to work, she saw an ad that said, "Travel to the USA as an au pair." That could be the way to go to America, she thought. She wasn't ready at the time she found the ad, but she saved it. Sally had a special box for all her personal items, and she placed the ad in it and waited for the right time to find out more information.

She asked God for a clear sign when it was time to move on.

A few months later, while attempting to open the door of the bar where she worked, the key didn't work. She peered through the window and saw a notice indicating bills and taxes hadn't been paid. The furniture was gone. The bar was closed. It was the clear sign she had been waiting for. She took the ad out of her special box and called the au pair agency.

Preparing information for the au pair agency was a six-month process. Applicants were required to be eighteen years of age, speak some English, gather ten personal recommendations, and pass a battery of tests on a variety of subjects. Once all that information was complete, the agency matched the au pair with a family.

Initially, Sally was matched with a family from Carmel, California. She spoke on the phone with the parents and the children. Her English was not that great at that time. One month before she was scheduled to leave, the family canceled because the mother lost her job, which meant the family could no longer afford an au pair.

Next, Sally was matched up with a family from the East Coast of the United States. She was led to believe the location wasn't too far from New York City. She was thrilled, but she knew she had to tell her mother, so Sally visited Mary one evening for dinner. They'd repaired their relationship by that point, and they were on good terms.

Not knowing how to tell her mother, Sally made small talk and then finally blurted out, "We have to talk. I am going to the United States. I have a job as an au pair through an agency."

Her mother began to cry, saying she was worried about Sally's safety.

Mary immediately called the agency to verify it was a legitimate venture. A photograph they took to commemorate the occasion tells the whole story: Sally has a huge smile, and her mother is crying.

Sally had a big party before she left for America. Friends and friends of friends celebrated Sally and her courageous spirit. One guy at the party was visiting relatives he knew from the bar where she had worked. He said he lived in the Pennsylvania area, gave her his card, and said she should call him when she was in the area.

Off on her next adventure, Sally flew into JFK airport, where she was immediately stunned by loud behavior. Croix-Rouge, France, was a place where everyone was polite and proper. When she got off the plane in New York and walked into the airport, a lady was yelling, "Passports! Passports! Go here! Go there!" The abrupt, loud behavior of the New Yorkers was a surprise and threw Sally off a bit. Getting through the airport took several hours, in addition to the eight-hour flight. She was exhausted, but she knew her family in France were anxiously waiting for her to call. At two o'clock in the morning, she found a pay phone, dialed, and heard cheering and a voice saying, "She made it! She made it."

Sally walked around the airport, trying to figure out where to get the shuttle bus to begin the next leg of her journey. She stopped at the information desk to ask where the ground transportation was, but with her limited English, the response sounded like "Blah, blah, blah." That didn't help at all. It took her a while, but she finally found the shuttle bus and the other people who were attending the au pair training in the city.

She had arrived. Her dream had come true! She admired all the lights and the buildings; she could hardly contain her enthusiasm and happiness.

It was March 2005. She checked into the New Yorker Hotel for one week of training organized by the au pair agency. Exhausted and jet-lagged yet excited, she dropped her luggage off in the room and wandered around until the wee hours of the morning. The first place she went was a famous fast-food restaurant, but she realized she didn't know how to order her meal in English. This was a big city she only knew from the movies. It felt like a dream. This was really where Sally wanted to be.

Sally enjoyed her week in the city, but anxiety crept in whenever she thought of the family she was going to in Connecticut. There she was, a twenty-one-year-old girl in a new country who couldn't really speak the language, taking an enormous risk.

At the end of the training week, Sally got on the train with all her luggage, not really knowing how long the trip was going to take. Three hours later, she arrived in the little town of Coventry, Connecticut. The mother of her au pair family, Jill, picked her up at the station. They recognized each other from the interview process, during which they'd exchanged photographs, and the meeting seemed to be a happy one for both of them, though Sally was somewhat disoriented; her head was spinning and confused about where she was and how different the people were.

Jill welcomed Sally with a hug and helped her with the luggage. As they drove through the small town, Sally thought, *What am I doing here?* They pulled into a driveway that seemed a mile long. The home was a mansion with six or seven bedrooms, an expansive yard, and an in-ground pool. The next thing they did was get Sally a Social Security card, the purpose of which was a mystery to her, and set up a bank account. To open the account, she needed a driver's license. Of course, she had been driving for years, but now she had to pass the driver's test in English. She passed.

Sally had a room of her own with a walk-in closet and her own bathroom, but she was not free. She had rules to follow. She was paid $600 a month, along with free room and board, but she had to cook, clean, and drive a fourteen-year-old boy wherever he wanted to go. When the boy was in school, she sat by the amazing pool, yet she was lonely. The arrangement seemed wonderful, especially since Sally came from a world of poverty, but she came to realize that one could have all the money one wanted, but if there was no one to share it with, it didn't matter. She was part homesick and part excited about the unknown. This feeling went on for a few weeks. The water, the air, and the food were different. It was as if she were on another planet.

In the end, the job was not to be. As it turned out, Sally was fired after four months because of miscommunications on both sides. Sally believed the weekends and evenings should be her free time, and Jill believed she should always be available.

Feeling a little betrayed, Sally thought, *Okay, what's next?* She knew two friends from France who were visiting Philadelphia, so she took the train to meet them there, where she would have someone to talk to and a place to stay. Her mission was to find somebody in America to help her out.

She was dedicated to staying in the United States and didn't want to tell her mom she'd gotten fired until she had a plan. Sally told me she finds it magical that when one is at the bottom and has nothing, one has to surrender to see what the universe is going to bring.

Sally had no reservations about seeking help in her effort to land a job. One of her friends suggested she call her former boss in France, where she had worked in a nightclub bar for three years as the main bartender. As it turned out, he had an uncle who lived and worked in Pennsylvania. Her former boss sent a note of introduction, telling the uncle to treat Sally "like a queen."

When Sally and her friends arrived at the restaurant, they met Gabe, the general manager, who welcomed Sally with a hug. He relayed the message he'd received and assured her she was in good hands. The owner of the restaurant was enamored with Sally and, especially, with her gorgeous blonde friends. They were given the use of a luxury condominium apartment during their stay. He took them to fancy restaurants in Philadelphia, and he took them shopping. The three of them lived like princesses. However, Sally knew that treatment was going to end when her friends went back to France, and it did, as predicted.

Sally had the promise of a job in the restaurant that was to begin in a few weeks. That gave her time to go back to France to close her au pair visa and return to the United States on a three-month tourist pass. She hoped to get into a school, which would allow her to stay on a student visa.

Upon returning to the United States, Sally looked for an apartment and eventually rented a basement room with a small bed, a little window, and a table for a total cost of one hundred dollars a week. Most likely, it was not a legal rental, but she didn't have much of a choice.

Recalling the man in France who'd given her his business card at her going-away party, Sally gave him a call, and it turned out he lived around the corner from her. They became good friends.

As they talked one night, he suggested she go to school to improve her English. She never had thought one could get a student visa simply for going to school to learn English, but Sally visited a school in her neighborhood and found out it was true. But there was one sticky requirement: she had to have $10,000 in a savings account before the school would sponsor her for a student visa.

How could she ever get that amount of money? Sally was making a hundred dollars a week, which barely paid her rent. There was no way except to talk to people she worked with at the restaurant, a long shot at best.

Sally found more angels. At the restaurant, a couple of her coworkers got together and helped her get all the documents and money she needed for the school. Upon returning to France, she applied for and was granted a five-year student visa.

Back in the States, it was time to really get to work. Sally desperately needed to earn enough money to live. She found another job at a restaurant in the city, and one day, while passing by the front of another restaurant, she saw through the window a white woman with long red hair belly dancing. Sally thought to herself, *Wait a minute. That's my culture. I know how to belly dance.* Belly dancing was something she'd learned at a young age, as she'd grown up going to weddings and parties where there was always dancing. It came naturally to Sally. She bought her first costume and contacted a few restaurants that might have some work for a dancer.

Three restaurants returned her call, and one hired her. She danced throughout Philadelphia and all the suburbs. Her popularity grew so fast she was able to buy her first car. It was not a new car, but it was new to Sally. She danced on weekends and worked in little shops and restaurants during the week.

While driving home after a dancing gig one day, she noticed a man in a fancy car trying to get her attention. After ignoring him for a short time, she finally opened her window. She said hello, and he told her she was beautiful and asked where she was from. She responded, "Egypt and France." He began speaking in French, and that was all it took. Sally was charmed. His name was David, and he was from an island where French was the native tongue. He was also a huge mistake.

Initially, David was attentive, texting and calling all the time. He showered Sally with gifts; flew with her first class to Florida; bought her Fendi boots, Gucci shoes, and a fur coat; and loaned her his Porsche. One day he invited her into his apartment in the center of the city. In the foyer was a big bouquet of flowers in the middle of the hallway, and he gave her the keys to the place. He was everything a girl could have wanted. Until he wasn't.

At the time, Sally was working as a hostess in a French restaurant. One day David told her she wasn't making enough money. He said she needed to work as a cocktail waitress. Sally was not happy, but David insisted that was where the money was. David knew a guy who knew a guy who could get Sally a job in a high-end restaurant and nightclub.

Sally took the job and made a ridiculous amount of money in the new job. Soon David started asking Sally to contribute to the rent. Then she discovered money was missing from her bag. Next, he started taking away the gifts he'd bought her. Sally happened to find the phone number of an ex-girlfriend of David. She decided to call the number, and the ex-girlfriend said, "Run. Run as fast as you can."

With that warning, Sally ran away from David with almost nothing in the bank. David appeared to be wealthy, but he was a scammer. Sally had to get a restraining order because he threatened her.

Sally moved to the opposite side of the city, where she lived, worked, and studied for the next three years. She went to college during the day and worked as a cocktail waitress until four o'clock in the morning five nights a week. In line with her entrepreneurial mindset, she also now had a belly dancing group that performed on the weekends.

Sally enjoyed the single life for three years and then met Walter. He was a sweetheart, and she fell in love quickly. Sally thought he was wonderful. In time, however, she began to notice strange behavior. He would disappear and wouldn't return her calls for days. When he did show up, he always had a seemingly good excuse. It took some time for her to realize he was an alcoholic. She knew she should leave him, but he was so nice, and he loved her so much. As a twenty-five-year-old young woman, she believed she could help him, especially because of her motivated, strong, and disciplined personality. In hindsight, she realized the more successful she was, the more depressed Walter became because he couldn't keep up with her.

Sally's life was again surrounded by turmoil. She started to gain weight and lose money because she had to spend time looking for and taking care of Walter. She didn't understand that alcoholism is a disease. She thought it was a choice. It was hard for her to comprehend how someone could do that to himself. It didn't matter if one's family was wealthy, middle class, or from poverty.

After picking Walter up from a drunken binge once again, Sally said to herself, *What am I doing? This doesn't feel like love.* Sally lamented that she didn't really know what love was, because growing up, she'd had no models to go by. It took time, but eventually, she couldn't even look at Walter any longer. She was finally done.

Sally always had wanted to become a US citizen, and after Walter, she thought it was time to pursue that dream. She thought about all the people she knew in the country from school and her work experiences. Again, with the help of an angel, she was guided in the proper direction to make her dream of becoming an American citizen come true. Sally was still going to school during the day and working at night.

Once Sally got her ten-year green card, she applied for citizenship. She studied hundreds of American history questions and answers most of a day waiting to be interviewed at the courthouse. Finally, she heard her name called and was asked to verify all the information on the certificate of citizenship, following that she correctly answered the American history questions. She was then told to go to another room straight ahead on the left. The room was like an intimate theater with about three hundred people inside. She found a seat and realized it was the citizenship ceremony itself. On the stage was a little stand with people from the government standing around it. They announced they had a message from the president of the United States. On the screen, Barack Obama began speaking. As Sally watched the video, she teared up and could not stop weeping. It was an emotional moment. Next, they called people up to the stage to receive their certificates of citizenship as the rest of the audience applauded. It was a big day! It was November 2014.

For Sally, success is personal. She explained to me, "It's not about impressing other people; it's proving to myself that coming from extreme poverty as an immigrant, I can still change the trajectory of where I am heading as a woman." Having an aptitude for business is important, and she believes learning about relationships is also an essential aspect of our lives. Sally considers herself a student of life, always continuing to grow while learning to be humble.

After years of working in restaurants and as a dancer, Sally launched a small digital marketing business. Her strong work ethic demanded nonstop effort. She even hired an employee to help achieve her goals. As time went by, she realized she needed to maintain balance in her life. She decided to sign up on a dating app to hopefully meet a good man. Nothing in her life thus far had prepared her for the next chapter in her adventure.

Sally met Eli online, and they developed a friendship in cyberspace that led to planning a quick meeting. The quick meeting became two hours of talking and walking around the center city. They met again a few days later for dinner, and over the weekend, they went to the beach. For a year, he supported her career, following her wherever she went.

Soon, however, red flags began waving, and Sally decided not to see them. After several months of dating,

Eli suddenly wasn't interested in spending time going out. If Sally wanted to go to a movie or out to dinner, he would agree and then would not contribute to the cost, saying he was saving money to buy a house.

Eli was focused on his desire to own a home and talked about how much more value they could get in New Mexico. Sally questioned why he wanted to go so far away, and he said, "I can make more money and pay less for a house, the weather is nice, and it's only a four-hour flight away."

Eli lived with his parents, so Sally suggested he move in with her to be closer to work. He said no. Sally didn't understand why he wanted to move across the country with her but not live with her in Pennsylvania. Red flag.

She began to question the scenario, yet she didn't want to lose him. Her next thought was *If we're not going to live together before we move across the country, let's go on a trip for a week to see how we get along.* Eli agreed and planned the trip.

Eli booked a trip to Europe. They fought constantly. In addition, when the credit card bill came in, she had no idea he would eventually ask her for her share of the $3,000 cost of the trip. Red flag.

As it turned out, Eli wanted to move because he had applied to join a police force in New Mexico. Sally was caught off guard and questioned why he wanted to be a cop. "What happens if you get shot?" Sally asked with genuine concern. She didn't want to lose him.

Eli said, "I want to help my country."

After dating Sally for almost a year, Eli received his acceptance letter to the police academy in New Mexico. He called her with the news and wanted her to move with him. Sally was driving at the time, and she pulled her car off to the side of the road and cried. She asked herself, *Is this what I'm supposed to be doing?* She'd fought hard to be self-sufficient while creating her marketing business.

After much soul-searching, Sally decided to go with Eli on the new journey. She drove with him twice across the country. During the drive, he calculated the hours of driving and turned to Sally when it was her turn. Even in the middle of the night, he woke her up and blurted out, "I drove two hours. Wake up. It's your turn to drive." He created a tabulation to record gas consumption, noting her share.

She heard the little voice in her head whisper, *I'm moving all the way to New Mexico for you, and you're charging me gas money?*

In addition, he told her on the trip west, "The rent is nine hundred dollars a month, which we will split fifty-fifty." Red flag.

In three months, Sally was nearly broke. She was looking for a job and trying to grow her own business in New Mexico but not making much headway. She was networking and meeting people every day. She spent hours at the library, building her contact list, and connecting with people over coffee. Everything cost money. Sally had only $700 in her bank account and asked herself, *How the hell did I get here?*

By December, Sally believed she was in some sort of depression, feeling sad and lonely. She didn't like where she was with Eli. They were fighting all the time. She was afraid to ask Eli for help in covering the rent for January. She had to get a job fast.

Sally always had worked hard, and now was not any different. She finally landed two jobs. Eli responded, "What? You're not going to be home to help me out?" Red flag.

As she was driving to work one day, Sally's car broke down. Eli told her she needed to get a new one. Sally wanted to repair her car, but Eli pushed her to get a new one. However, he refused to cosign for a loan. While she was car shopping, the salesman asked, "Why isn't he cosigning for you? Didn't you drive cross-country for him?" She left the dealership with deep anxiety. Red flag.

Sally was beginning to realize her relationship with Eli wasn't in her best interest. Sensing her mistrust in him, Eli hooked her when he said, "Let's start looking for a house!"

They had good moments while they were house hunting, holding hands and being lovey-dovey.

In Sally's heart, she knew New Mexico was not where she wanted to be. She loved to travel and wanted to see the world. She didn't know why she'd convinced herself this was happiness. Feeling stressed out, Sally and Eli had a huge fight, and Eli left the house and did not return until the next day. He never said where he had gone. The silent treatment went on for days.

Sally received a message from a woman on her website that said, "Guess where Eli slept last night?"

Sally eventually learned the woman was someone Eli had met on a dating site. She stalked Sally, calling her forty times a day.

Sally was distraught and decided it was time to make a move out of the house. She packed up most of her things and put what fit into her car. She stayed at a friend's overnight. The next day, she rented a truck and packed up the rest of her things alone in the heat of the day, which took about ten hours. Her adrenaline kept her going.

Eventually, Eli came home and saw the house empty. He called her. She was crying behind the steering wheel of her car when he asked, "What are you doing?" He told Sally, "I told my mom that I was going to marry you and that you were the one for me. I love you. Come home, please. I bought this house for us. There's an extra room for our children. I can't see my life without you."

What did Sally do? She went back. She wanted to go back.

In phone calls and letters, her family and friends in France expressed their concern for her, so she decided to visit them. They gave her some much-needed love and, after hearing her story of making terrible decisions about romantic partners, recommended she read books on manipulative behavior.

Psychology Today describes psychological manipulation as the deliberate creation of an imbalance of power and the exploitation of the victim to serve an agenda. Sally read that there are fourteen signs of manipulation, including silent treatment, isolation, cheating, playing dumb, and lying, to name a few. All were examples of Eli's behavior and the behavior of Sally's earlier men. Another form of manipulation is gaslighting, a deep form of manipulation that makes one doubt herself and question her own memory. For example, Eli once said, "Let's go to the movies."

Sally responded, "When do you want to go?" Eli said, "Tonight at eight."

Sally responded, "I have to work. Let's go at noon tomorrow. I'll meet you at home."

"Okay." Both agreed.

The next day, Sally was home at noon, waiting for Eli. She called him and asked where he was, and he said, "I'm at the movie theater."

Sally responded, "But we said we were going together at noon." Eli replied, "No, you told me you were working."

Sally's family and friends loved her too much to allow her to continue to be blinded by Eli. Learning about his behavior by reading about other similar relationships opened her eyes to her reality. Sally believes sometimes girls who don't have a father figure have a difficult time sorting out love on their own, as she did. There is a lot of falling down, getting up, falling down again, and getting back up again to understand a healthy romantic relationship. Raising one's standard comes from feeling worthy.

It is important to know everyone is worthy of respect and love.

Today Sally is again living her dream, and she feels free. She travels freely and can work from anywhere as a nomadic digital marketing entrepreneur. Sally is passionate about being an immigrant and being a woman in this wonderful country of America. She is working on a book featuring female immigrant entrepreneurs. She hopes her story inspires other women to do what they know in their heart is the right thing to do.

How does Sally endure? With strength, determination, and love.

Break Free

I only want to die alive,
never by the hands of a broken heart.
I don't wanna hear you lie tonight now
that I've become who I really am.

This is the part when I say I don't want it. I'm stronger than I've been before. This is the part when I break free, 'cause I can't resist it no more.[7]

This next story was written by my dear friend Linda for inclusion in this book on hope. We met twenty years ago at a music class, when our boys were just a few months old. Our friendship continues to grow. I am honored that she shared her story with me and is sharing it with you, the reader.

The strongest people are not those who show strength in front of us but those who win battles we know nothing about.

Unknown

8

LINDA

A Story of a Family's Tragedies and Finding Strength in Love

Sitting on my dad's knee was the best feeling in the world. In that minute, I was the only person in the room and in the center of the sun. I was special. In that minute, I felt confident. I felt safe. Looking back, I know I felt loved.

But a few years later, hiding in the dark in the backyard, behind bushes, with my mother and brother Brian, trying to see into the kitchen to see what my dad was doing—he was drunk again—the feeling was different. I was frustrated with the fighting and pissed off at my mom for having us hide in the yard to spy on my dad. I was sick of all of it—the drinking, the fighting, the craziness. By the age of nine, I was tired of it.

It was interesting to grow up in an alcoholic family in the suburbs. From the outside, we looked like the perfect family in the perfect house, including an in-ground swimming pool and a basketball hoop in the driveway, with a bunch of teenage boys shooting baskets. Kids rode their bikes for hours on end and played in the woods, building forts. But there were two realities: the reality of going to my brother's soccer games, watching my mom talk to all the other moms, and playing with the kids over on the other side of the field and the nighttime reality of waiting for my father to come home, knowing my mother was sitting at the table just waiting. When he finally arrived, it all began: the rage, the yelling, the shoving, and the feeling of dread while it continued.

People thought my brother Brian and I were twins because I was so tall for my age. We shared a bedroom early on, and we'd whisper to each other, wondering when our parents would stop fighting. Wondering if our dad was going to come upstairs and go after one of us. Wondering why our mom wouldn't just go to bed and leave him alone. Sometimes our older sister, Susan, would come in and say funny things to make us laugh and relieve the fear. Other times, she'd stay in her room. But most often, she'd go downstairs to try to break up the fight. I never understood why she'd get involved. *Stay out of it, Susan*, I'd think. *Let them kill themselves.* More often than not, in trying to break it up to keep the peace and protect them from themselves, she'd end up the victim—a sixteen-year-old girl getting hit by a six-foot, 190-pound construction worker.

I was the youngest of five children. I grew up in the suburbs. We walked to our elementary school around the block and spent summers at the beach, where my mom taught swimming classes. My best friend, Paddy, and I spent days playing with our two brothers in the woods, building forts and climbing trees. We always played at Paddy's house; it was an oasis. Her mother stayed home and did occasional volunteer work at the library. Because her father was a doctor, they had a lifestyle very different from ours, including sleep-away camps, piano lessons, acting lessons, and a maid. I often fantasized about living in her house and being adopted by her parents. Her mother was a soft-spoken woman from the Midwest and was always kind to me, always attentive, and compassionate. Somehow, she knew things were not right in my home; she knew about the troubles. Her attention was a gift.

My parents were working-class people. Both were the children of immigrants and had grown up in a city environment. Moving out to the suburbs was a working-class dream, and my parents worked hard. Work was a family value. With five children, they both managed to go to college and earn bachelor's degrees and, eventually, master's degrees. My mom became a teacher, and my dad worked his way up in the union to become an official.

There was violence off and on throughout my childhood. Smacking kids had been perfectly acceptable when my parents grew up. That was what they'd been taught. Unfortunately, that behavior, fueled with alcohol, got out of control.

I had two other older brothers, Sean and Ryan. I adored them. The two of them were as thick as thieves. Sean was a quiet guy, and Ryan was a firecracker and charmer and always with a different girl. As quiet as Sean was, Ryan was equally outgoing. They were opposite sides of one coin.

Sports was the other family value. Everyone played sports, or you weren't really part of the gang. If you were good, you got attention. My sister, Susan, and brother Ryan were both outstanding athletes, earning the attention of our parents. My brother Sean was not. Quiet and not athletic, he faded in the glow of Ryan, the athlete and charmer. Ryan, always the independent one, went off to college on a baseball scholarship. Sean also went to school but soon dropped out and returned home. He was unable to find a job. When I look back now, I think Sean was depressed early on, but no one noticed—too many kids, too much overtime to try to get ahead, and too much alcohol.

It's a sad story. When I look at pictures of us as kids, I see the beautiful faces of intact, healthy, cute kids. There was no predicting what the future would hold for us.

My brother Brian and I were two years apart and younger than our other brothers and sister. As a result, we were our own team. Brian was never able to live up to Ryan's legacy as an athlete in town (strike number one), he was very smart (strike number two), and he was very sensitive (strike number three). Early on, a neighbor friend could see he was struggling and advised my parents to get him counseling. The fighting and the abuse were taking a toll.

But counseling was something for someone else—maybe for rich people but not people from our background. You didn't go to strangers and tell them your troubles. You toughed it out and moved on. That was the only option. There were no other choices allowed.

As the youngest of five kids, I was able to go unnoticed. I was not a great athlete but did okay in school and stayed out of trouble. I knew I was loved by my brothers. My sister, on the other hand, had to be my parent. She was an authority figure. She was the one everything fell to: making dinner for us at night when my mother took classes at the local college, cleaning on the weekends, doing laundry, and more. Always the responsible one, it was as if Susan had kids when she was a teenager: a little brother and sister she had to parent. She had no choice, and it was not a lot of fun.

Yet there was another side of the family story: camping trips when we were little, a boat for my brothers when they turned fifteen and sixteen, a pool installed when I was twelve, and lots of parties with Dad's friends from the union and all their kids. When Susan was sixteen, she wanted to take guitar lessons, and my parents allowed me to join her—two for the price of one. (I'm sure Susan was thrilled—more to sacrifice for the sister-child.) My parents wanted us to have opportunities they'd never had, and in that opportunity, I found something I was good at: music. By fourth grade, I added French horn to the guitar, and by fifth grade, I was getting standing ovations at local recitals. A little girl playing guitar and singing folk songs was unexpected.

Paddy had a piano, and I played it when I was at her house. Her mother knew I had talent and tried to talk my parents into getting a piano for me. It took three years before they agreed and before they could afford it. What an indulgence. It was the most expensive thing in our house. My parents told me, "We will never tell you to practice. If you don't practice, it goes."

That was the deal, and I kept the deal. I practiced like crazy and was brought to a teacher who fed me with praise. I performed in competitions and recitals. She had me convinced I would become a great pianist one day, and that became my dream. Music gave me an identity and an outlet. It was something to pour my feelings into.

Things continued to deteriorate with my father. After his mother died, he went on a terrible drinking binge and wound up being hospitalized for depression. Of course, we didn't understand any of it. When he came out of the hospital, there were promises that the drinking was over. He went to Alcoholics Anonymous. My mom went to Al-Anon. All would work out.

My sister had stayed home for her first two years of college so she could continue to take care of Brian and me while Mom finished taking classes. Susan moved out with a boyfriend and continued taking classes. Ryan lost his baseball scholarship due to drinking, and Sean left for the navy in search of a trade and a new life. Brian and I were left with my parents, and the drinking started again.

My father never connected with my brother Brian. He went after him when he came home. For whatever reason, he seemed to see his failures in Brian, the son he could never connect to. There were nights when I went into Brian's room to try to comfort him, but I was the younger sister, the baby, and it was a role I didn't know how to play. By the time I was ten, I had completely stopped communicating with my father in any way. We never spoke. I somehow thought if I could punish him enough, he would understand how much he was hurting us and would finally stop drinking. Years passed with no communication. Things got worse. And Brian changed.

What our neighbor had warned would happen slowly happened. As Brian got older, he got angrier, and he too started down the road of drugs and alcohol. By the time he was sixteen, my mother threw him out of the house. He dropped out of high school, and I was the only one left. When things got bad, Susan would take me to her apartment. By then, my parents had put me into an all-girls religious school. They were terrified I would follow in Brian's footsteps. They wanted to protect me from all the outside influences they blamed for his troubles. Unfortunately, they didn't understand that damage had already been done.

I felt out of place at school. I arrived there at the beginning of junior high school and didn't know anyone. I still had the piano and my teacher, and they were my anchors. I eventually became friends with three sisters who lived near me. High school was the beginning of drinking and smoking pot for me and my friends. The weekend started on Thursday night, when their parents would go out. Because they were a well-known family in town—they were members of the church, and their father was a doctor—I was allowed to spend huge amounts of time at their house. Once again, I found myself fantasizing about being in another family. Their mother also was kind, somehow knew things were not right in my home, and showed me compassion.

I wanted to dislike the new school but somehow knew it was a good place for me. I developed close relationships with two of my teachers, whom I respected and loved. Once again, there was interest shown in me, attention given to me, and time spent on me, and once again, they somehow knew that things were not right in my life. Again, I received the gift of compassion.

It was hard to live in two worlds: a world of chaos and hurt that filled me with rage at home and a world at school that spoke of forgiveness and love and showed me love and compassion.

I was sitting on the bus next to my friend Carol one day, heading home from school in tenth grade, and I mentioned that it had been more than two weeks since we had seen or heard from my brother Brian. Once again, he had visited the house and drank while he was there. When my mom had come home that night, she once again had thrown him out. He never returned to my brother Ryan's house, where he had been living. No one knew where he was.

A day later, I returned home from school and found my sister's boyfriend, Bob, out on the driveway. Cars were in front of the house. Bob grabbed me as I walked up the driveway. Sobbing, he told me that Brian had been found dead, lying in the woods along the side of the railroad tracks. Susan was still at the police station. My parents were in the house. Bob just kept crying. I just stood there on the driveway, knowing in that moment that everything had changed forever. How I could know that at sixteen, I'm not sure. But I was right. Things were never the same.

I was unable to deal with my parents; the rage was so intense. I held them responsible for Brian's suicide. The only two adults I could speak to were my two teachers from school. Those were the people I called. I knew I could trust them. I knew there would somehow be love there to receive.

At my brother's funeral, the line went out the door and down the block. We were a big family from a small town. So many people I didn't know and didn't care about. My friends and I were alienated from all of it. My sister, Susan, had to identify the body, and it was a closed-casket wake. He had been lying in the woods for two weeks. At his burial, I stood alone away from the family. I couldn't look at them. I was dazed and disappearing into grief.

My friend's mom saw me standing there alone and came to me. She put her arms around me. I remember that like it was yesterday. No one had ever hugged me like that. I gave off too much anger for anyone to hug me like that. That one act of simple kindness and human compassion was unlike anything I had ever experienced.

My dad and brothers drank. I smoked pot. My sister handled the arrangements. I avoided my mother. We all went off into separate corners and anesthetized ourselves. There was nothing else I could do to manage the anger and the pain. One of Brian's friends had his leather jacket and gave it to me. I couldn't take it off. I wore it to the wake. I wore it to the funeral. I wore it to the burial. I couldn't take it off. I had never felt so alone. My twin was gone.

I was desperate to get away. My aunt from the West Coast asked if I would like to stay with them for a while, but my mother said no. I was trapped in that house with people I hated and blamed for my brother's death. My mother wanted me to go to school the day after the funeral. I refused. When I returned to school a week later, I felt alone and completely different from every girl there. I felt as if there were echoes inside my body—the emptiness was echoing.

My father's drinking got worse after Brian's suicide. I started smoking more pot and drinking to stop the anger. I ran away and slept in friends' basements and doorways in town. After a week, I called home, and my mother, crying, said she was going to leave my father. She begged me to come home. I refused. She told me she was leaving him and said I could go with her. I refused. She said she would talk to Carol's parents to see if I could stay there for a while. My mom left, and I moved out. My father was left alone.

He went back to AA and started going to meetings every day. My mom went back, and eventually, I returned. My father begged my forgiveness. I kept smoking pot. My parents put me in therapy, but I had been taught never to go outside the family and never to tell anyone our business. The therapy stopped after a couple of months with no changes for me. Just anger simmering.

Piano continued and was the only thing I cared about. My goal became to go to college and get away from all the pain—and I did. Two years later, I left for college and excelled. I went to a small state college, and after the first year, a professor told me I didn't belong there. That professor took an interest in me. He invited me to his house for dinner with his family. He saw something in me that I couldn't see. He said, "You should be down in New York City at a great school. You can do better than this. Apply to a university."

I had no idea what he was talking about. I'd never seen myself as anything special. But he did. He pushed me to study abroad and to transfer to a better school. The work ethic my parents had instilled kicked in, and I continued to excel. Unfortunately, the music department included talented kids from other countries, and I quickly realized I was never going to be able to compete at that level on piano, so I changed majors. I followed my teacher's suggestion and left to study in France.

I'll never know where my determination to survive came from. I'd like to think it came from God. I'd like to think the people in my life who had shown me compassion and love were angels or gifts that fed my soul.

After studying in Europe, I enrolled at a university in New York, a much more competitive school, and I thrived. In spite of drinking and getting high, I maintained the work ethic I had been taught and continued to excel academically.

By then, my sister, Susan, had finished graduate school and was working at the World Trade Center as an engineer. Both my brothers were working for the union. Ironically, my siblings were all drinking too much, but my dad was still sober. My relationship with my father was slowly improving, although it took years before we could even have a conversation.

When I returned home for Thanksgiving break in my junior year, I learned there was a new crisis. My brothers had torched a car while under the influence of alcohol, in retaliation after the owner of the car hit our dad at work with brass knuckles, shattering his jaw. It was a stupid thing, and a district attorney eager to make a name for himself publicized the incident and went after the greatest penalty. It didn't look good, and it wasn't. My two brothers were sent to jail. They had no prior arrests and no prior legal history and had committed a drunken act. A great story for the district attorney.

They separated my brothers and moved them three times. At every jail they went to, the inmates would burn them out by setting fire to their beds and belongings. The inmates thought they were undercover cops. My one brother was kept downstate, where my family could visit him. My other brother was sent upstate, where no one could visit him easily. I made a point of driving to the prison, and I will never forget my brother's condition when I saw him.

I had never seen a person look hunted. He couldn't look at me. He kept looking around. He couldn't sit still. He was smoking nonstop, terrified. He didn't belong there. He was a pawn in a game he'd had no idea even existed. What could I say to him? "Be strong"? "Hang in there"? "Things will get better"? What words could help him? There were none. How could I leave him there? The bell went off when the visiting time was up, and I walked out, thinking for the first time in my life that he might not be okay. I didn't know what that meant, but I knew he was in trouble.

Again, I returned to school, thinking I was different from all my friends. I felt alone again and isolated, not knowing how to integrate that reality with the rest of my life. My two brothers were in jail, and I was off to class. I felt guilt, anger, and fear for my brothers.

The following year, my brothers were released. They had survived. Ryan had developed a heart problem and was supposed to stop drinking and smoking. He tried and failed. He and Sean both went back home to their wives, and things returned to some semblance of normalcy. They went back to work. My sister was living close to her place of work, the World Trade Center, and I started my senior year at college. I was getting ready to study again in Europe. I had been awarded a PhD fellowship at Northeastern University and would attend when I returned from my studies abroad. I was accomplishing things no one else in our family ever had. I was happy and excited about the future.

The summer before Europe, I got a job at a coastal resort in Rhode Island and moved there with a friend to work, save money, and have fun. I worked two jobs and chased boys in between.

When a call from my father came, I couldn't imagine what it was about. He never called me. Our routine was that I would call home collect every Sunday to let them know I was okay. I walked out to the pay phone across the street and dialed my parents' house. When my dad answered the phone, I didn't recognize his voice.

"You have to come home, Linda. You have to come home. You have to get on a plane and come home."

My brother Ryan had died of a heart attack in his sleep as a result of a congenital defect.

How could this have happened again? What family lost two sons? Again, we went to the same funeral parlor. Again, the line was out the door and down the street. My father was devastated. My mother was numb. My brother Sean was heartbroken, and Susan was devastated. The situation was surreal.

I must have gone to another place emotionally. I remember little. What I do remember is my brother Sean. It was as if he had lost himself. I had no idea how he would survive without Ryan. They had done everything together; they'd worked together and helped build each other's home. How would the quiet man survive without his best friend and brother?

I went back to school to finish my last semester before Europe, but that had become an empty idea. The excitement and romance of the trip were gone. I started leaving college every weekend, driving long distance to be with my sister. I just wanted to be with my siblings—and drink. And that was what I did. I visited my sister every weekend, and we went out and drank. Then I met a man to drink with.

I went to Europe, as scheduled, and was miserable. I wanted to be home. I wanted to be with my sister and the man I had met. All the excitement was gone. I just wanted to be with my family.

The PhD fellowship was still waiting for me when I returned, so I went to Northeastern, as planned. I had to keep working—family value number one. I got an apartment in the city and tried to study. I could not. I had lost my focus. I had lost my ability to concentrate. I was depressed but didn't know it. I took a leave of absence from the university and went to work. I drove back and forth between Boston and New York, drinking all weekend with my new boyfriend. I had fallen in love with someone who had more problems than I did. I eventually got a new job up in Boston, where I had to be on call with a beeper. I could be called into work at any time. A friend had the nerve to tell me I'd better stop drinking or I would lose my job. *Fuck you*, I thought.

But she was right, and I couldn't afford to lose the job. So I tried to stop drinking.

A couple from Ireland lived across the street from me in Boston. I used to chat with them on the street from time to time. I loved the man because he worked construction and reminded me of my brothers. He had a thick Irish accent and a wonderful sense of humor, and we became fast friends. I had seen a copy of the AA *Big Book* on the dashboard of his car. He knew I was struggling not to drink. One day, over coffee, he invited me to try a meeting. "If you don't like it, we'll be happy to refund your misery," he said. As a friendly gesture, he put his hand out to me, and we shook hands. "There is a place for you, Linda," he said. Once again, I received compassion and kindness.

One meeting led to another and another. I had dinner at his house with his wife on Friday nights. He helped me change my life.

I moved down to New York to be with my fiancé. However, I quickly realized I had a decision to make: recovery or the relationship. He continued to drink and couldn't get sober. I knew the relationship had to end. I was fighting to survive. I ended it after things got worse and violence started to erupt. I could not go back to that kind of life after all I had gone through.

My heart was broken, and I was stuck in New York. I wanted to go back home to Boston, where I had gotten sober and had friends who loved me.

I kept attending meetings and working and thought about returning to school. Time passed, and I met someone. Jim was a sweet, kind man who did not drink. I started therapy. It was hard. I didn't know how to be in a relationship. My AA sponsor and my therapist pulled me through much of the fear I had. Again, I received compassion from two people. And love. Always love.

I decided it was time to go back to school. I missed learning and studying. I needed to do something that meant something to me. I no longer wanted to write economic policy and work for the government, removed from the people I was trying to help, people I would never get to see. Instead, I decided I wanted to help people directly, the same way I had been helped. I applied to graduate school for social work.

Jim and I moved in together. I went to school. We got engaged. I graduated and got a job. Things were really different for the first time in my life. I was sober; in a healthy, loving relationship; and building back my relationship with my family. I was working hard on all my pain and anger through therapy. I was in a place no one in my family had ever been in. I was living a life different from everything I had ever been exposed to. Jim and I married, starting on a path together.

A year later, we had a baby. Our son, James, was the greatest joy of my life, bringing new life and new hope.

I worked part-time in the evenings after we had our

son, so I could be home with him all day until he went to school. It was a privilege I loved. I continued to go to therapy, wanting to learn how to be a different kind of parent. A son was a scary thing for me. I thought about my brothers and needed to know it could be different.

While playing with James one morning, I got a call from my dad, who said, "You have to get here. We're at the hospital. Your brother's in the emergency room. He had a heart attack at work." He too had the congenital heart problem that ran in the family. "Find Susan, and get here."

Surely this couldn't be. He'd be okay. He was in the hospital. We'd get there and see him, and everything would be all right. He just had to hold on. He had to not give up. I thought, *Just get your sister. Just get Susan. Get her, get over there, and everything will be all right.* He couldn't possibly leave us. He had two little boys. He just had to hold on until we got there, and he'd see. He couldn't leave.

When we got to the hospital and started toward the doors, Sean's wife came out. She was sobbing. "He's dead. He's gone."

"What? That can't be," I said.

"He's gone. It was his heart. It just gave out."

My sister passed out right there on the sidewalk in front of the hospital.

People came running. "Get her inside! Check her heart!"

I stood there not believing. It couldn't possibly be right. I went into the hospital and found my mother. She was sitting there crying. Where was my dad? I needed to find my dad. He'd said to get there quickly. It couldn't be. I'd kept praying Sean would hold on. I'd thought he'd hold on. But I'd gotten there too late. I'd been too slow. It had taken me too long. I should have gotten there sooner.

My father finally came out of two swinging gray steel doors, surrounded by men from the job. He looked directly at me and said, "My last son is gone. He's gone. I have no more sons."

I just looked at him. How could this possibly be? Who could lose three children? It just couldn't be.

My brother left behind two little boys, Sean and Ryan, the next generation. Watching the boys learn the news was one of the hardest things I'd ever had to witness. They were unable to understand it. They hid like two little wounded animals. They looked haunted. It was excruciating.

Next came another wake, another funeral, another burial, and another goodbye. Too many goodbyes. The boys became our priority. We had to love the boys through the tragedy, and that became our work: to help the boys. We had to find them a therapist to work with, help get them settled financially, and go visit as often as possible. It was something to focus on, something to work on in the midst of all the despair.

Of course, I had my own little boy. I thanked God for the distraction. I saw family every weekend, staying as close as possible after more loss. Every weekend, we tried to be together.

My sister really started to struggle after that. I convinced her to get therapy. She went into a profound state of depression. I had her at my house all the time. I needed to hold on to her. I couldn't stand any more loss. We just held on to each other and the children and waited for the pain to pass.

We spent every weekend and every holiday together after that. My parents would come to me if Susan and I couldn't get out to them. James became the joy of the family, something positive and hopeful. Time passed. One year. Two years. Three years. James was ready to start preschool.

But something was not quite right. Although James was happy and engaged, he was not speaking much and didn't always look at us. My sister said something about it. She was scared. I hated her for saying it out loud. I was scared. We scheduled an appointment at a local pediatric center.

Our assessment was scheduled for Tuesday, September 11, 2001. James was three years old. My husband's sister and I pulled into the underground parking garage at the hospital and headed toward the elevators. Two Hasidic Jewish men were on the elevator, talking about some sort of attack. Something about terrorists. I assumed it was in Israel.

When we got to our floor and walked into the assessment center, I saw a television showing a picture of the World Trade Center. It was a little before nine o'clock, and a plane had hit one of the towers. I quickly thought of my sister, Susan, and knew she wasn't at work yet; she always went in a little after nine. Plus, she worked in the North Tower, and the accident had occurred in the South Tower. We went in and started the assessment.

About an hour later, we left the room and walked out. People were standing around the television. The other tower had been hit. I called my sister-in-law in the suburbs. "Did you talk to Susan?"

"She's in the tower!" My sister-in-law was hysterical.

I grabbed James and ran to my car. I was driving and calling people when the news announced that the South

Tower had collapsed. I made it home and called my husband. The news was on. The North Tower had collapsed.

My parents were on the road, traveling. They couldn't get home because all major highways were shut down. The airports were shut down. Everything was shut down. My neighbor across the street who worked at the Trade Center came home; she'd made it out.

"Did you see Susan?" I asked her. "No," she said simply.

I heard no word from anyone. I called everyone who knew Susan. Nothing. No one knew anything. Never for a minute did I think she was dead.

I called her boss, who said, "Susan's a fire-safety engineer; she knew what to do. We just have to wait."

We waited. My parents finally got to my house. We watched the news, seeing thousands of people make it out of the towers. It would just be a matter of time before we heard from her.

The next day, I got up at three o'clock in the morning and started driving to the area hospitals. I went to three hospitals, and no one knew anything. No wounded ever had come. We continued to wait and were reassured that she had probably gone down into the PATH station, knowing it would be safer.

We waited another day, and then my father and I went into the city to find her. I will never forget the pictures of the faces of the missing. Everywhere. Faces of people hanging from chain-link fences. Hanging on every wall. More and more faces. We were not allowed anywhere near the site. We were told to go to the Armory, where they had information for the families. We went and sat and waited. We heard there had been thousands of body bags ordered. Thousands. Where were all the missing people? Where was my sister?

I believed she had gone underground, as her friend had said, and thought it was just a matter of time until they found her and others.

"How long could she last under there?" I'd asked.

"Probably up to two weeks with the food stores. We have to just wait," her friend had said.

After two weeks, my parents said it was time. Time to say goodbye.

Again. My sister was never recovered.

I had to start taking medications after Susan's death. I was battling anxiety and depression that were dragging me under. The pull from the dead was starting to feel stronger than the pull toward life. I had to stop working.

I tried to take care of my son and had to put him in school full-time while I helped my parents. My husband's family helped with my son. I went from being the youngest of five children to being an only child. My parents were destroyed. The only thing that kept me above water was my son.

I'm still recovering from the loss of my siblings and will always be recovering. The wounds no longer bleed, but terrible scars remain. The blessing of my son was the only thing I could hold on to after I lost Susan. The blessing of my son got me through two bouts of cancer and, later, heart disease. The love of my husband and my son have been the greatest gifts of my life.

What happened in our family was unnatural and inexplicable. I rarely tell my story, because it is too much for most people to hear. I'm telling it here in the hope that someone else might understand that we have an incredible survival instinct and that it only takes little bits of love to keep us alive. That is the thing that helped me endure. From way back, someone always was there to offer me some small gift of compassion and love that allowed me to hold on.

Years later, I now have a wonderful career, and I still have the love of my husband and my son. I have helped many children, many adults, and many families over the course of my work. I have tried to use the power of love and compassion in all I do. It has always served me well.

I often think of the nuns from my school, the moms of my friends, my teachers, my mentors, and the people in recovery who showed me love and compassion when I needed it. I fall back to a line in John 4:8: "God is love."

How does Linda endure? Love and compassion.

Angels among Us

When life held troubled times and had me down on my knees,
There's always been someone to come along and comfort me.
A kind word from a stranger, to lend a helping hand.
A phone call from a friend just to say, "I understand." But
ain't it kind of funny, at the dark end of the road, That
someone lights the way with just a single ray of hope?

Oh, I believe there are angels among us,
Sent down to us from somewhere up above.
They come to you and me in our darkest hours
To show us how to live, to teach us how to give,
To guide us with the light of love.[8]

CONCLUSION

All of the incredible people in these stories shared their personal journey to help others in similar circumstances know they are not alone. Their kindness and generosity of spirit make me want to be a better person. Learning about other people's lives has brought more awareness of the struggles people endure throughout life.

I discovered one constant in all the people who shared their stories in this book: love. Love might come from a stranger, a family member, or a friend, but having love is the key to surviving. Love is described in the New Testament of the Bible:

Love is patient, love is kind. It does not envy, it does not boast, it is not proud. It does not dishonor others, it is not self-seeking, it is not easily angered, it keeps no record of wrongs. Love does not delight in evil but rejoices with the truth. It always protects, always trusts, always hopes, always perseveres. Love never fails. But where there are prophecies, they will cease; where there are tongues, they will be stilled; where there is knowledge, it will pass away.

And now these three remain: faith, hope and love. But the greatest of these is love.

My hope is for

- a widow to know that life goes on, though it might need to be taken one day at a time;
- someone who has lost a loved one to have the power to rise up each day continue on;
- scientists to find cures for incurable diseases;
- no one to be hungry;
- people to be kind to each other;
- love to conquer hate;
- peace instead of war;
- justice over injustice;
- help, not hurt;
- people's values to be determined by their character and not by their ge the color of their skin, or their nationality; and
- everyone to understand we are all part of the human race in this world together.

We all feel, and we all have hurt. Find a ray of sunshine to spread light and love to others.

A last thought to reflect on is best stated by Morrie Schwartz. In the book, "Tuesday's With *Morrie,*" Mitch Albom writes about his conversations with his college professor Morrie, who was losing his battle with ALS.

Morrie believed the most important things in life had "to do with love, responsibility, spirituality and awareness."

Morrie's last words were "As long as we can love each other, and remember the feeling of love we had, we can die without ever really going away. All the love you created is still there. All the memories are still there. You live on—in the hearts of everyone you have touched and nurtured while you were here."

Imagine

Imagine no possessions.
I wonder if you can.
No need for greed or hunger.
A brotherhood of man.
Imagine all the people sharing all the world.
You,
you may say I'm a dreamer,
but I'm not the only one.
I hope someday you'll join us,
and the world will be as one.[9]

Middle school and high school students combined efforts to communicate this message of hope to a high school where a school shooting took place.

ENDNOTES

1 Nat King Cole, vocalist, "Smile," by Geoffrey Claremont Parsons, Charles Chaplin, and John James Turner Phillips, track 6 on *Ballads of the Day,* Capitol Records, 1956.

2 "Here Comes the Sun," by George Harrison, the Beatles, track 7 on *Abbey Road*, Concord Music Publishing, 1969.

3 Rihanna, vocalist, "Diamonds," by Sia Furler, Mikkel Eriksen, Tor Hermansen, and Benjamin Levine, *Unapologetic,* Def Jam Recordings and SRP Records, 2012.

4 Andy Williams, vocalist, "The Impossible Dream," by Joe Darion and Mitchell Leigh, side 3, track 1 on *The Impossible Dream*, Capitol Records, 1971.

5 Mariah Carey, vocalist, "Hero," by Mariah Carey and Walter Afanasieff, track 2 on *Music Box,* Capitol Records, 1993.

6 Mariah Carey and Whitney Houston, vocalists, "When You Believe," by Stephen Schwartz, Arista Records, 1998.

7 Ariana Grande, vocalist, "Break Free," featuring Zedd, by Martin Max, Savan Kotecha, and Anton Zaslavski, track 5 on Ariana, *My Everything*, Republic Records, 2014.

8 "Angels Among Us," by Don Goodman and Becky Hobbs, track 11 on Alabama, *Cheap Seats*, RCA Records, 1993.

9 "Imagine," by John Lennon and Yoko Ono, track 1 on John Lennon, *Imagine*, Apple Records, 1971.

www.ingramcontent.com/pod-product-compliance
Lightning Source LLC
LaVergne TN
LVHW041848070526
838199LV00045BA/1500